Mindful Love

Strategies to Fix Overthinking in Your Relationship

LEE M. HANSEN

This report aims to provide precise and robust information on the issue and the issue secured. The output could be rendered with the prospect of the manufacturer not needing to do bookkeeping, officially licensed or otherwise eligible administrations. Should an exhortation be relevant, lawful, or qualified, a rehearsed individual in the call should be required. The Statement of Principles was approved and endorsed by the American Bar Association Committee and the Publications and Associations Commission. It is not lawful to reproduce, copy, or distribute any portion of this study using either electronic methods or the community written. The registering of this delivery is deliberately disallowed, with the exception of written distributor authorization, the ability of this material is not permitted. All resources are retained. The information provided is conveyed to be truthful and consistent, in so far as any chance, in the absence of thinking or something else, of any usage or misuse of any methods, procedures, or cookies found within is the special and definite responsibility of the receiver per user. Any civil duty or liability shall be put upon the seller for any reparation, damage, or moneyrelated misfortune attributable to the data received, whether explicitly or indirectly. Those authors assert all copyrights which the seller does not retain. The statistics herein are solely for instructional purposes and are all. The details were reached without consent or acknowledgement of guarantee. The markings used shall be without permission, and without the approval or help of the proprietor of the label shall be published. All logos and trademarks in this book are for information purposes only and are held explicitly by individuals who are not affiliated with this document.

LIMITED LIABILITY - DISCLAIMER

The contents of the book titled "Mindful Love Strategies to Fix Overthinking in Your Relationship" are provided for informational purposes only. The author and publisher make no representations or warranties regarding the accuracy, applicability, completeness, or suitability of the information contained within this book.

The information presented in this book is based on the author's personal experiences, research, and opinions. It is not intended as professional advice and should not be considered as such. Readers are encouraged to consult with qualified professionals for advice tailored to their specific situations.

The author and publisher shall not be held liable for any direct, indirect, consequential, special, exemplary, or other damages arising from the use of the information provided in this book. This includes, but is not limited to, damages for loss of profits, data, or other intangible losses.

The author and publisher do not endorse or assume any responsibility for the content of external websites or resources referenced in this book. The inclusion of such links does not imply endorsement or approval of the content, views, or opinions presented on these external sites.

Readers are responsible for their own actions and decisions based on the information presented in this book. The author and publisher disclaim any liability for the outcomes of such actions or decisions.

By reading this book, readers acknowledge and agree to the limited liability and disclaimer outlined herein. If readers do not agree with these terms, they should not use the information provided in this book.

This limited liability disclaimer is subject to change without notice. It is the responsibility of readers to review and be aware of any updates to this disclaimer.

By accessing and using the information in this book, readers accept and agree to the terms and conditions outlined in this limited liability disclaimer.

TABLE OF CONTENTS

Introduction: Navigating Overthinking in Relationships

Introduce the concept of overthinking in relationships and its impact

In the intricate dance of love, where emotions weave a tapestry of connection, there exists a subtle but potent force that often creeps into the sacred space between two individuals - overthinking. In the realm of relationships, overthinking is more than a mere mental exercise; it is a complex cognitive pattern that can significantly influence the dynamics of love. As we embark on this exploration of mindful love strategies, it is imperative to first comprehend the nuanced nature of overthinking and the profound impact it can have on the delicate fabric of a relationship.

Overthinking in relationships is a cognitive phenomenon wherein individuals find themselves trapped in an incessant loop of analyzing, dissecting, and overanalyzing various aspects of their connection with their partners. It's a mental state where the mind becomes a battleground of doubts, uncertainties, and a barrage of 'what ifs.' The seeds of overthinking can be sown by myriad factors, ranging from past traumas and insecurities to societal expectations and personal fears. The human mind, in its quest for understanding and certainty, can inadvertently plunge into the labyrinth of overthinking, jeopardizing the simplicity and purity that love inherently embodies.

The impact of overthinking on relationships is profound and multifaceted. At its core, overthinking breeds a sense of constant unrest, casting a shadow over the blissful moments that relationships are meant to cultivate. It erects barriers to open communication, as individuals become hesitant to express their true thoughts and feelings, fearing the potential repercussions of their partner's reactions. The spontaneity that often characterizes the early stages of love can be stifled by the looming presence of overthinking, transforming what should be a joyful journey into one fraught with tension and doubt.

Moreover, overthinking can engender a distorted perception of reality, where benign actions and innocent words are subjected to meticulous scrutiny, leading to unnecessary misunderstandings and conflicts. It becomes a self-fulfilling prophecy, where the doubts generated by overthinking manifest into tangible issues within the relationship. This constant mental chatter can erode the foundation of trust, replacing it with a fragile edifice of suspicion and anxiety.

In essence, the impact of overthinking on relationships extends beyond the psychological realm; it reverberates through the emotional and even physical dimensions of love. The stress and anxiety induced by overthinking can manifest as a palpable strain on one's well-being, influencing everything from sleep patterns to overall mental health. Relationships, once a source of solace and support, can become unwitting sources of stress, as the tendrils of overthinking infiltrate every interaction, casting a shadow over the potential for genuine connection.

As we delve into the strategies to counter overthinking and cultivate mindful love, it is essential to recognize that overcoming this intricate challenge requires a holistic approach. It involves not only addressing the symptoms but also understanding the root causes that give rise to overthinking in the context of relationships. By shedding light on this phenomenon and acknowledging its impact, we set the stage for a transformative journey towards a more mindful and fulfilling love.

Importance of mindfulness as a tool to address overthinking

In the intricate tapestry of human emotions, where the threads of love and connection weave together, the practice of mindfulness emerges as a powerful and transformative tool. When it comes to navigating the complexities of relationships and combating the pervasive influence of overthinking, mindfulness stands as a beacon of awareness and presence. In this exploration of mindful love strategies, it is crucial to delve into the profound importance of mindfulness as a nuanced and effective approach to address the incessant chatter of overthinking that often plagues romantic connections.

Mindfulness, at its essence, is the art of cultivating a heightened awareness of the present moment without judgment. It beckons individuals to embrace the richness of each experience, fostering a deep connection with oneself and others. As we unravel the layers of overthinking and its impact on relationships, the role of mindfulness becomes increasingly evident—a steadying force that allows couples to break free from the chains of incessant mental rumination and rediscover the simplicity and beauty inherent in shared moments.

One of the primary contributions of mindfulness to the realm of relationships lies in its ability to anchor individuals in the present. Overthinking often pulls individuals into the treacherous waters of the past or propels them into an uncertain future, breeding anxiety and doubt.

Mindfulness serves as a lifeline, pulling couples back into the embrace of the now, where authenticity and connection flourish. By fostering a conscious awareness of thoughts and emotions as they arise, mindfulness provides a buffer against the relentless tide of overthinking, offering couples the opportunity to respond to each other from a place of clarity and presence.

Furthermore, mindfulness acts as a potent antidote to the destructive cycle of overthinking by encouraging non-judgmental observation. In the crucible of a relationship, misunderstandings can escalate when overthinking attaches negative interpretations to innocent actions or words. Mindfulness invites individuals to witness their thoughts without immediately accepting them as truths. This pause for reflection allows couples to discern whether the mental narratives fueling overthinking are grounded in reality or distorted by ingrained fears and insecurities. In this way, mindfulness becomes a discerning lens through which the tangled web of overthinking can be unraveled.

Crucially, the practice of mindfulness fosters emotional intelligence, a cornerstone of healthy relationships. By attuning individuals to the ebb and flow of their own emotions, mindfulness lays the groundwork for empathetic understanding of a partner's inner world. In the face of overthinking, where assumptions and misinterpretations can run rampant, this heightened emotional intelligence becomes a bridge for effective communication. Couples equipped with mindfulness are better equipped to navigate the stormy seas of conflict, approaching disagreements with a compassionate curiosity that transcends the limitations imposed by overthinking.

Moreover, mindfulness extends its influence beyond the realm of conscious thought, permeating the very fabric of how individuals engage with their partners. It promotes active listening, a skill that is often drowned out by the clamor of overthinking. As couples learn to listen with presence and intention, they create a space for authentic communication, where vulnerabilities can be shared, and misunderstandings dissolved. Mindfulness, therefore, becomes a relational superpower, dismantling the barriers erected by overthinking and paving the way for genuine connection.

Set the tone for the book, emphasizing the transformative power of mindful love in fostering healthier relationships

In the vast landscape of love, where hearts entwine and souls seek connection, this book emerges as a guide, a compass navigating the delicate intricacies of relationships. As we embark on this journey together, the overarching theme that will resonate through every page is the transformative power of mindful love—a force that has the potential to not only mend the fractures caused by overthinking but to elevate relationships to new heights of understanding, connection, and fulfillment.

At the heart of this exploration lies the recognition that love, like any intricate masterpiece, requires mindful attention and deliberate intention. It is a call to arms for individuals seeking not just to coexist in relationships but to thrive, to flourish together in a shared space of authenticity and vulnerability. The transformative journey we are about to undertake transcends conventional relationship advice; it is an invitation to cultivate a love that is not only enduring but deeply enriching.

The tone of this book is one of optimism, underpinned by the unwavering belief that love, when approached with mindfulness, becomes a catalyst for personal and relational growth. It is an antidote to the prevailing narratives that depict relationships as inherently tumultuous or destined to succumb to the pressures of modern life. Instead, we celebrate the inherent resilience of love and its capacity to evolve into a source of strength and inspiration.

The transformative power of mindful love is rooted in its ability to break the chains of habitual overthinking, a common malady that often plagues relationships. Overthinking, with its insidious whispers of doubt and anxiety, can cast a pall over the most beautiful unions. This book serves as a beacon of hope, asserting that the antidote to overthinking is not found in complicated relationship maneuvers or quick fixes, but in the profound simplicity of mindfulness.

Mindful love is not a passive state but an active, intentional practice. It involves a conscious commitment to being present, both with oneself and with a partner. It calls for a departure from the autopilot mode that often governs our interactions, encouraging individuals to engage with the richness of each moment. The transformative journey begins with a shift in perspective—from viewing love as a destination to understanding it as a dynamic, evolving process that requires ongoing nurturing and attention.

As we navigate the chapters ahead, each page is an opportunity to delve into the myriad ways mindfulness can be infused into the fabric of a relationship. From communication strategies that foster understanding to the cultivation of emotional intelligence, the transformative power of mindful love unfolds in practical, actionable steps. This is not a theoretical treatise but a hands-on guide, offering readers the tools they need to embark on their own journey of relational transformation.

The tone is one of encouragement and empowerment. Mindful love is not an elusive ideal reserved for a select few but a potential that resides within the grasp of every individual willing to embark on the journey. It acknowledges the imperfections inherent in human connections, emphasizing that growth and transformation are not synonymous with perfection. Instead, it celebrates the beauty of the messy, unpredictable, and wonderfully human aspects of love.

In essence, this book sets the tone for a narrative of hope, resilience, and the boundless potential of love when approached with mindfulness. It is an affirmation that relationships are not static entities but living, breathing entities capable of adapting, growing, and thriving. The transformative power of mindful love awaits, promising a journey that transcends the confines of overthinking and opens the door to a realm where love flourishes in its purest and most authentic form.

Chapter 1: Understanding Overthinking in Relationships

Nature and causes of overthinking in the context of romantic relationships

In the intricate tapestry of romantic relationships, the phenomenon of overthinking emerges as a shadowy figure, casting its influence over the delicate dance of connection. To truly understand the impact of overthinking, we must embark on an exploration of its nature and delve into the roots that allow it to take hold within the context of love. The complex interplay of emotions, past experiences, and societal expectations forms the backdrop against which overthinking unfolds, leaving individuals entangled in a web of doubt and uncertainty.

At its core, overthinking in romantic relationships is a cognitive process characterized by the repetitive and obsessive analysis of various aspects of the relationship. It extends beyond the normal considerations that accompany thoughtful reflection, morphing into a relentless cycle of second-guessing, dissecting, and scrutinizing every nuance of interactions with a partner. The origins of overthinking are as diverse as the individuals who experience it, but common threads often lead back to deep-seated insecurities, past traumas, and societal pressures that create a breeding ground for the incessant mental chatter.

One prominent factor contributing to overthinking in relationships is the baggage of past experiences. Unresolved issues or traumas from previous relationships can cast a long shadow, influencing how individuals perceive and approach their current romantic connections. A history of heartbreak or betrayal can give rise to a heightened vigilance, causing individuals to overanalyze every gesture or word from a current partner in an attempt to protect themselves from potential pain.

Societal expectations also play a significant role in nurturing the seeds of overthinking. The pressure to conform to societal norms regarding the ideal relationship can lead to a constant comparison with external standards. Individuals may find themselves questioning the authenticity of their connection, wondering whether it aligns with the societal narrative of what love should look like. This external pressure introduces an element of self-doubt that fuels the overthinking cycle.

Moreover, personal insecurities can act as fertile ground for the growth of overthinking. Whether stemming from childhood experiences or societal messages about self-worth, insecurities can magnify perceived flaws and create a distorted lens through which individuals view themselves and their partners. The fear of not being 'enough' or the worry of being unconditionally loved can trigger a cascade of overthinking, as individuals grapple with their own perceived inadequacies.

Communication breakdowns within a relationship can also contribute to the proliferation of overthinking. When open and honest communication is lacking, assumptions and misinterpretations can flourish. Individuals may fill in the gaps with their own narratives, often veering towards negative interpretations that fuel the overthinking cycle. This lack of clarity becomes a breeding ground for unnecessary doubts and anxieties.

The nature of overthinking in romantic relationships is, therefore, multifaceted—a confluence of internal and external factors that create a perfect storm of doubt and anxiety. It is crucial to recognize that overthinking is not a sign of inherent relationship flaws but rather a manifestation of complex internal and external influences. By understanding the roots of overthinking, individuals can begin to untangle the web it weaves, paving the way for a more authentic and grounded connection.

As we navigate the complexities of overthinking in romantic relationships, it becomes evident that the first step towards overcoming this challenge is self-awareness. By recognizing the patterns and triggers that fuel overthinking, individuals gain the agency to interrupt the cycle. This self-awareness lays the foundation for a more intentional and mindful approach to love—one that is not overshadowed by the constant hum of overthinking but grounded in the present moment and the authentic connection between partners.

Impact of overthinking on communication, trust, and emotional well-being

In the delicate ecosystem of romantic relationships, the impact of overthinking manifests like ripples on the surface of a tranquil pond, disrupting the clear waters of communication, trust, and emotional well-being. To comprehend the extent of its influence, we must explore how overthinking permeates these vital elements, distorting the landscape of connection and leaving a trail of challenges in its wake.

Communication, the lifeblood of any thriving relationship, bears the brunt of overthinking's influence. The incessant mental chatter that characterizes overthinking creates a barrier to open, authentic dialogue. As individuals become entangled in a web of doubt and second-guessing, the clarity of communication diminishes. Simple expressions of love or gestures of care may be scrutinized, misinterpreted, or, in some cases, withheld altogether due to the fear of potential repercussions. The unspoken assumptions bred by overthinking become a silent wedge, driving a subtle but impactful wedge between partners.

Trust, the bedrock upon which healthy relationships are built, faces erosion in the face of overthinking. The constant questioning of motives and intentions, fueled by the relentless cycles of overanalysis, breeds an atmosphere of suspicion. Overthinkers may find themselves scrutinizing every interaction for hidden meanings or ulterior motives, undermining the foundation of trust that is essential for a robust connection. Trust requires a certain level of vulnerability and belief in the good intentions of a partner, qualities that can be compromised when overthinking takes center stage.

Emotional well-being, intimately tied to the health of a relationship, becomes a casualty of overthinking. The mental gymnastics involved in overanalyzing every word and action can lead to heightened stress and anxiety levels. The emotional toll is not confined to the overthinker alone; it permeates the relationship, creating an atmosphere of tension and unease. Emotional well-being thrives in an environment of security and mutual understanding, qualities that are often sacrificed on the altar of overthinking.

Moreover, the impact of overthinking on emotional well-being extends beyond the immediate emotional landscape. It can have tangible effects on physical health, disrupting sleep patterns, elevating stress hormones, and contributing to a general sense of fatigue. The toll of overthinking on emotional and physical well-being becomes a vicious cycle, as compromised well-being further fuels the propensity to overthink, creating a self-perpetuating pattern of distress within the relationship.

The implications of overthinking on communication, trust, and emotional well-being highlight the need for intentional and mindful strategies to counter its influence. Effective communication, grounded in openness and vulnerability, becomes a crucial antidote to the communication breakdowns induced by overthinking. Couples can benefit from cultivating a space where honest expression is encouraged, and the fear of misinterpretation is mitigated through active listening and mutual understanding.

Rebuilding trust necessitates a conscious effort to address the root causes of overthinking. Partners can work collaboratively to create an environment where transparency and honesty are valued, assuaging the doubts that overthinking may breed. This involves not only verbal reassurances but also consistent actions that align with the shared values and expectations of the relationship.

Prioritizing emotional well-being within the relationship involves a holistic approach. Both partners can engage in self-care practices that promote mental and physical health, reducing the fertile ground for overthinking to take root. Additionally, fostering a supportive atmosphere where emotional vulnerabilities are met with empathy rather than judgment can create a resilient foundation for the well-being of both individuals and the relationship as a whole.

Insights into common triggers and patterns associated with overthinking in love

In the intricate tapestry of love, overthinking often emerges as an unexpected intruder, casting shadows on the canvas of connection. Understanding the common triggers and patterns associated with overthinking in the realm of love is pivotal to unraveling its complexities. As we delve into the intricate landscape of romantic relationships, we encounter a myriad of influences that can ignite the overthinking spiral.

One of the primary triggers for overthinking in love is rooted in past experiences, particularly those laden with emotional intensity. Past heartbreaks, betrayals, or instances of rejection can leave indelible imprints on an individual's psyche, creating a psychological minefield that is activated in the context of new relationships. The fear of history repeating itself becomes a fertile ground for overthinking, as individuals find themselves scrutinizing their current partners for any perceived signs of impending heartache.

Societal expectations, often internalized through cultural norms and media portrayals, constitute another potent trigger for overthinking in love. The pressure to conform to idealized notions of romance and relationship milestones can lead individuals to constantly assess their relationships against external benchmarks. Comparisons with societal ideals can spawn doubts about the authenticity or adequacy of one's own relationship, fostering a breeding ground for overthinking.

Insecurity, both personal and relational, is a pervasive trigger for overthinking in love.

Insecurity about one's self-worth or attractiveness can fuel thoughts of unworthiness, prompting individuals to question why their partners would choose to be with them. Relational insecurity, marked by a fear of abandonment or a sense of inadequacy in meeting a partner's needs, can similarly contribute to overthinking as individuals grapple with the perceived fragility of their connections.

Miscommunication or lack of clarity within a relationship serves as a common trigger for overthinking. When partners fail to express themselves openly or when messages are ambiguous, individuals may fill in the blanks with their own interpretations. The resulting uncertainty becomes fertile ground for overthinking, as the mind attempts to construct narratives to make sense of the ambiguity.

Patterns of overthinking often manifest in certain recurrent themes. Catastrophizing, a cognitive distortion where individuals envision the worst-case scenarios, is a prevalent pattern associated with overthinking in love. This may involve imagining the end of a relationship based on minor disagreements or interpreting benign actions as signs of impending disaster. Catastrophizing magnifies uncertainties, contributing to heightened anxiety within the relationship.

Another common pattern is incessant reassurance-seeking, where individuals habitually seek external validation from their partners. This behavior stems from a need to alleviate the anxieties generated by overthinking, but it can inadvertently strain the relationship by placing undue pressure on the partner to continually affirm their commitment and love.

Overthinkers may also engage in a cycle of self-doubt, constantly questioning their own worthiness of love. This pattern can lead to a self-fulfilling prophecy, where the persistent doubts undermine the individual's confidence and contribute to behaviors that strain the relationship.

Understanding these triggers and patterns is crucial in developing strategies to mitigate the impact of overthinking in love. It requires a blend of self-awareness and open communication within the relationship. Individuals can benefit from recognizing their personal triggers and cultivating mindfulness to interrupt the overthinking cycle when it begins.

Moreover, partners can work collaboratively to create an environment where open communication is encouraged, and fears and insecurities can be shared without judgment. Establishing a foundation of trust and mutual understanding helps to alleviate the triggers associated with past experiences and societal expectations, fostering an atmosphere where love can thrive authentically.

Cognitive-behavioral techniques, such as reframing negative thoughts and challenging catastrophic thinking, can be instrumental in breaking the patterns of overthinking. Developing a more balanced and realistic perspective allows individuals to approach their relationships with greater clarity and resilience.

Chapter 2: The Mindfulness Approach: Cultivating Presence in Love

Introduce mindfulness as a therapeutic approach to address overthinking

In the realm of combating overthinking, mindfulness emerges as a potent and transformative therapeutic approach, offering a path towards greater self-awareness, emotional regulation, and a profound shift in perspective. As we navigate the labyrinth of thoughts that often entangle individuals in the web of overthinking, introducing mindfulness becomes not just a suggestion but a guiding light toward a more intentional and fulfilling way of engaging with one's inner world and, by extension, with the complexities of romantic relationships.

Mindfulness, at its core, is a practice rooted in present-moment awareness. It involves cultivating a non-judgmental, accepting stance towards one's thoughts and emotions. The essence of mindfulness lies in being fully present, embracing each moment with a sense of curiosity and openness. In the context of overthinking, mindfulness acts as a counterforce, disrupting the habitual patterns of rumination and providing individuals with the tools to step back from the incessant mental chatter.

One of the fundamental tenets of mindfulness is anchored in the breath. As individuals learn to anchor their attention to the rhythmic flow of breath, they create a stable foundation in the present moment. This anchoring effect becomes particularly relevant in the context of overthinking, where the mind tends to wander into the past or project into an uncertain future. By returning to the breath, individuals ground themselves in the now, breaking the cycle of overthinking and fostering a heightened awareness of the present.

Mindfulness encourages a gentle observation of thoughts and emotions without attachment or aversion. Instead of being swept away by the current of overthinking, individuals learn to observe their thoughts as they arise, acknowledging them without being defined by them. This non-attached awareness allows for a more objective evaluation of thoughts, reducing the emotional charge that often accompanies overthinking.

The practice of mindfulness also extends to the body, bringing attention to physical sensations and the felt experience of emotions. Often, overthinking is accompanied by physiological manifestations such as tension, restlessness, or a sense of unease. Mindfulness invites individuals to explore these sensations with curiosity, allowing for a deeper understanding of the mind-body connection. By becoming attuned to bodily sensations, individuals gain valuable insights into the triggers and patterns associated with their overthinking tendencies.

Furthermore, mindfulness emphasizes the concept of acceptance, encouraging individuals to embrace their experiences without judgment. In the context of overthinking, this involves acknowledging that thoughts are transient and not necessarily reflective of reality. Through the lens of mindfulness, thoughts are viewed as passing clouds in the sky of consciousness—ephemeral and ever-changing. This shift in perspective fosters a sense of self-compassion, allowing individuals to navigate the terrain of overthinking with greater kindness towards themselves.

The application of mindfulness in addressing overthinking within romantic relationships involves both individual and collaborative practices. Individually, mindfulness provides a toolkit for individuals to manage their own overthinking tendencies. Couples can also integrate mindfulness practices into their shared experiences, fostering a collective journey towards a more mindful and harmonious connection.

Mindful communication becomes a cornerstone in the relational application of mindfulness. By bringing a non-judgmental and present-moment awareness to conversations, couples create a space where each partner feels heard and understood. Mindful listening involves giving one's full attention without immediately formulating a response, allowing for a more authentic exchange of thoughts and emotions.

Mindfulness in relationships also involves cultivating gratitude and appreciation for the present moment. Couples can engage in shared mindfulness practices, such as meditation or mindful walks, to enhance their connection and create a reservoir of positive experiences that serve as a counterbalance to the challenges posed by overthinking.

The therapeutic benefits of mindfulness extend beyond the immediate alleviation of overthinking. Research indicates that regular mindfulness practice contributes to changes in the brain associated with improved emotional regulation, heightened empathy, and enhanced overall well-being. As individuals and couples embrace mindfulness as a way of being, they not only address the symptoms of overthinking but also embark on a transformative journey towards a more resilient and flourishing relationship.

Principles of being present in the moment and non-judgmental awareness

In the fast-paced and ever-evolving tapestry of modern life, the principles of being present in the moment and cultivating non-judgmental awareness stand as beacons of mindfulness—profound guides to navigating the complexities of the human experience. As we embark on an exploration of these principles, we uncover the transformative power they hold in reshaping our relationship with time, thoughts, and the rich tapestry of emotions that color our lives.

Being present in the moment, a fundamental tenet of mindfulness, invites individuals to anchor their awareness in the current slice of time, disentangling themselves from the web of past regrets or future anxieties. It is an intentional choice to inhabit the now, recognizing that the present moment is the only moment that truly exists. In the context of overthinking, which often thrives on revisiting past scenarios or forecasting potential futures, the practice of being present becomes a powerful antidote.

The essence of being present lies in cultivating a heightened awareness of one's surroundings, sensations, and thoughts. It involves embracing the richness of each moment with a sense of curiosity and openness, much like a traveler immersing themselves in the unique sights and sounds of an unfamiliar landscape. By attuning attention to the present, individuals create a refuge from the mental whirlwind of overthinking, fostering a more grounded and centered state of being.

Non-judgmental awareness, the second cornerstone of mindfulness, complements the practice of being present by encouraging individuals to observe their thoughts and emotions without attaching labels of 'good' or 'bad.' It is a shift from the habitual tendency to evaluate experiences through the lens of judgment, allowing for a more impartial and accepting stance towards the ebb and flow of the mind.

In the context of overthinking, which often involves a cascade of self-critical or judgmental thoughts, non-judgmental awareness becomes a transformative tool. It involves recognizing that thoughts are fleeting and do not define one's identity. Rather than being entangled in a web of self-blame or condemnation, individuals can observe their thoughts with a compassionate detachment, acknowledging them as passing phenomena in the stream of consciousness.

The practice of non-judgmental awareness extends beyond thoughts to encompass emotions and sensations. Embracing emotions without judgment involves acknowledging them without immediately categorizing them as positive or negative. This nuanced approach allows individuals to explore the full spectrum of their emotional landscape, recognizing that each emotion has its own unique wisdom and significance.

Practicing non-judgmental awareness also involves bringing attention to physical sensations without assigning them value judgments. Whether experiencing tension, relaxation, warmth, or coolness, individuals can observe these sensations with a gentle curiosity, recognizing them as part of the ever-changing tapestry of the present moment. This mindful attention to the body serves as an anchor, grounding individuals in the immediacy of their physical experience.

The principles of being present in the moment and non-judgmental awareness are interwoven threads that create the fabric of mindfulness. They synergistically work together, amplifying the transformative impact on individual well-being and the quality of interpersonal relationships.

The application of these principles extends beyond formal meditation sessions into the fabric of daily life. Mindful moments can be woven into routine activities, such as savoring the flavors of a meal, appreciating the warmth of sunlight, or fully engaging in a conversation without mental distractions. By infusing these principles into the tapestry of daily existence, individuals foster a more vibrant and conscious way of living.

In relationships, being present in the moment becomes a gift—one that communicates attentiveness, validation, and a genuine connection with a partner. The art of non-judgmental awareness in relationships involves approaching interactions with an open heart, free from preconceived notions or the burden of past judgments. This creates a space where partners can authentically express themselves without fear of condemnation, fostering a deeper and more intimate connection.

Moreover, these principles offer a resounding invitation to break free from the shackles of overthinking within relationships. The act of being fully present dismantles the habit of projecting into an uncertain future or dwelling in the shadows of past grievances. Non-judgmental awareness disrupts the cycle of self-critical thoughts and encourages a more compassionate and understanding perspective, both towards oneself and one's partner.

Mindfulness exercises and techniques for cultivating presence in romantic relationships

Cultivating mindfulness within romantic relationships is a transformative journey that involves intentional practices to foster presence, deepen connection, and navigate the intricate dance of love with greater awareness. By incorporating mindfulness exercises and techniques into the fabric of daily interactions, couples can create a shared space that nurtures authenticity, understanding, and a profound sense of being present in each moment.

1. **Breath Awareness in Shared Moments:** *Exercise:* Begin by finding a quiet moment together. Sit comfortably, close your eyes, and focus on your breath. Notice the inhale and exhale, allowing your breath to anchor you to the present moment. As you breathe, bring awareness to the sensations of being together. Notice the shared space, the warmth, and the connection between you two.

Intention: This exercise not only grounds you in the present moment but also enhances the sense of togetherness. Sharing the experience of breath creates a subtle but profound connection, fostering a deeper understanding of each other's presence.

2. **Mindful Listening:** *Exercise:* Set aside dedicated time for open communication. One person speaks while the other listens without interruption or judgment. Afterward, the listener reflects back what they heard, ensuring a mutual understanding.

Intention: Mindful listening encourages a present-moment focus on your partner's words. It fosters a deeper connection by creating a space where each person feels truly heard and understood, fostering trust and intimacy.

3. **Gratitude Journaling Together:** *Exercise:* Set aside a few minutes each day to write down things you appreciate about each other. Share your entries and discuss them together. Focus on specific moments or qualities that enhance your connection.

Intention: Gratitude journaling shifts the focus to the positive aspects of the relationship, fostering a sense of appreciation. This exercise promotes mindfulness by redirecting attention away from potential stressors or overthinking and towards the richness of shared experiences.

4. **Sensory Awareness Exercise:** *Exercise:* Choose a simple activity, such as preparing a meal or taking a walk. Engage

all your senses—notice the colors, textures, scents, and sounds. Share your observations with each other, deepening your connection through sensory awareness.

Intention: This exercise encourages mindfulness by bringing attention to the sensory aspects of shared experiences. By engaging together in the present moment, couples create a shared tapestry of sensory richness, enhancing their connection.

5. **Loving-Kindness Meditation for Each Other:** *Exercise:* Sit together comfortably and close your eyes. Begin with a few minutes of shared silence, then focus on sending loving-kindness to each other. Silently repeat phrases like "May you be happy, may you be healthy, may you be safe, may you be at ease."

Intention: Loving-kindness meditation deepens the sense of connection by fostering feelings of warmth and goodwill. This practice encourages a shift from overthinking to a heart-centered awareness, enhancing the emotional bond between partners.

6. **Technology-Free Quality Time:** *Exercise:* Designate specific times when you commit to being technology-free. Engage in activities together without the

distraction of phones or screens, allowing for undivided attention to each other.

Intention: Disconnecting from technology fosters presence by eliminating external distractions. It creates a space for genuine, undistracted interaction, promoting a deeper understanding of each other.

7. **Body Scan Exercise:** *Exercise:* Lie down comfortably together and take turns guiding a body scan meditation. Bring awareness to each part of the body, starting from the toes and moving up to the head. Notice any tension and consciously release it.

Intention: The body scan exercise promotes a heightened awareness of physical sensations, promoting relaxation and connection. By sharing this practice, couples deepen their understanding of each other's physical and emotional well-being.

8. **Shared Mindful Activities:** *Exercise:* Engage in activities that naturally invite mindfulness, such as gardening, cooking, or art. Pay close attention to each step of the activity, savoring the process together.

Intention: Shared mindful activities provide an opportunity for joint presence and creativity.

Focusing on the activity at hand allows couples to break free from the mental clutter of overthinking and engage with each other in a more profound way.

Incorporating these mindfulness exercises into the rhythm of daily life can profoundly transform the quality of romantic relationships. They offer practical tools for staying present, deepening connection, and fostering a shared journey of growth and understanding. As couples embark on this mindful exploration together, they lay the foundation for a relationship that flourishes in the richness of each moment, free from the entanglements of overthinking and grounded in the authenticity of shared presence.

Chapter 3: Communication Breakdown: Overcoming Misinterpretations

How overthinking can lead to misinterpretations and communication breakdowns

In the intricate dance of human interaction, overthinking can emerge as a silent disruptor, casting shadows over the clarity of communication and paving the way for misinterpretations and breakdowns in understanding. To grasp the impact of overthinking on communication, we must embark on an exploration of how the incessant mental chatter can distort messages, create assumptions, and ultimately hinder the fluid exchange of thoughts and emotions within relationships.

Overthinking, with its relentless cycle of rumination and analysis, can give rise to misinterpretations by introducing a filter of subjectivity through which individuals perceive communication. As thoughts spiral into complex webs of doubt and uncertainty, the original intent behind a message can become obscured. A seemingly innocuous statement or action may be overanalyzed, leading to interpretations that align more with the overthinker's internal narrative than with the sender's actual intention.

Furthermore, overthinking often involves a heightened sensitivity to perceived cues or nuances in communication. Microexpressions, subtle changes in tone, or even the choice of words can take on exaggerated significance in the mind of an overthinker. This hypersensitivity can lead to the magnification of minor details, distorting the intended meaning and paving the way for misinterpretations that may veer far from the true essence of the message.

The tendency to create narratives in the absence of clear information is a hallmark of overthinking. When faced with ambiguity or gaps in communication, overthinkers may fill in the blanks with their own assumptions and projections. These self-generated narratives can deviate significantly from reality, leading to a skewed understanding of the message and potentially sparking unnecessary anxiety or conflict.

Communication breakdowns, rooted in the soil of overthinking, often manifest in the form of assumptions and unspoken expectations. As overthinkers grapple with their internal dialogue, they may project their fears, insecurities, or preconceived notions onto the communication with their partner. This projection creates a disconnect between what is said and what is perceived, setting the stage for misunderstandings that can strain the fabric of a relationship.

The overthinker's mind, entangled in a web of constant analysis, may also struggle to fully engage in the present moment. Active listening, a cornerstone of effective communication, becomes a casualty as the mind becomes preoccupied with internal dialogue and interpretation. This lack of attentiveness can result in important details being overlooked or misunderstood, contributing to a breakdown in the exchange of information and meaning.

Moreover, the impact of overthinking on communication is not confined to the interpretation of spoken words alone. Non-verbal cues, which play a crucial role in conveying emotions and intentions, can be misread when viewed through the lens of overthinking. A simple gesture or facial expression may be subject to layers of interpretation, leading to misunderstandings that stem from the overthinker's internal landscape rather than the reality of the moment.

The insidious nature of overthinking is that it can create a self-perpetuating cycle. As misinterpretations and communication breakdowns occur, they fuel the overthinker's belief that their fears and anxieties are justified.

This reinforcement can deepen the overthinking habit, exacerbating the challenges in communication and potentially eroding the foundation of trust within the relationship.

Addressing the impact of overthinking on communication requires a multi-faceted approach. First and foremost, cultivating self-awareness is essential. Individuals need to recognize the patterns of overthinking, including the triggers that prompt their internal analysis. This awareness forms the basis for breaking the automaticity of overthinking and creating space for more intentional and present communication.

Active communication strategies also play a crucial role in mitigating the effects of overthinking. Partners can establish open and honest dialogue about their communication styles, preferences, and potential pitfalls. This includes expressing the need for clarity, reassurance, and the creation of a safe space where concerns can be addressed without judgment.

Mindfulness practices, such as staying present in the moment and cultivating non-judgmental awareness, offer valuable tools for counteracting overthinking. By consciously redirecting attention to the immediate context of the conversation, individuals can minimize the intrusion of overthinking and foster a more direct and authentic exchange of thoughts and emotions.

Furthermore, setting clear expectations and practicing active listening can serve as antidotes to communication breakdowns induced by overthinking. Clarifying intentions, expressing feelings openly, and seeking confirmation when in doubt contribute to a shared understanding that transcends the distortions introduced by overthinking.

Role of mindful communication in resolving misunderstandings

In the intricate landscape of human connection, misunderstandings are an inevitable part of the journey. However, the way we navigate and resolve these moments of miscommunication can profoundly impact the health and resilience of our relationships. Mindful communication emerges as a guiding light in this process, offering a pathway to understanding, empathy, and constructive resolution when misunderstandings arise.

At the heart of mindful communication lies a commitment to being fully present in the interaction. This presence involves a conscious awareness of the current moment, free from the distractions of past grievances or future anxieties. When faced with a misunderstanding, approaching the conversation with mindful presence creates a space where both parties can engage in a more intentional and focused dialogue.

Mindful communication also emphasizes active listening—a skill that holds the power to transform the dynamics of a conversation. Rather than merely hearing words, active listening involves a deep and empathetic engagement with the speaker's message. Mindful listeners strive to understand not only the content of the words but also the emotions, intentions, and unspoken nuances behind them. This empathetic listening lays the groundwork for a more accurate and compassionate interpretation of the message.

In the context of misunderstandings, the role of mindful communication becomes particularly crucial. Instead of reacting impulsively or defensively, individuals engaged in mindful communication pause to reflect on their own thoughts and emotions. This reflective stance allows for a more measured response, reducing the likelihood of escalating tension or exacerbating the misunderstanding.

Mindful communication invites individuals to become attuned to their own emotional landscape and to express themselves authentically. This involves a careful examination of one's feelings, needs, and concerns before articulating them to a partner. By articulating emotions with clarity and vulnerability, individuals contribute to a shared understanding, creating an environment where misunderstandings can be unraveled with greater ease.

Moreover, mindful communication encourages individuals to approach misunderstandings with curiosity rather than judgment. The inclination to judge, fueled by assumptions and preconceived notions, can hinder the resolution process. Instead, a curious mindset invites open-ended questions, a willingness to explore different perspectives, and a genuine interest in understanding the intricacies of the other person's experience.

Mindful communication also places a spotlight on non-verbal cues and body language. These subtle expressions often convey emotions that words alone may not capture. Being attuned to these non-verbal signals enhances the depth of understanding and allows individuals to perceive the emotional nuances that might otherwise be overlooked.

In the resolution of misunderstandings, the practice of "checking in" becomes a valuable tool within mindful communication. This involves periodically pausing the conversation to confirm that both parties are on the same page. Clarifying and summarizing the key points of the discussion helps to ensure that the intended message has been accurately received, reducing the potential for ongoing confusion.

Additionally, incorporating mindfulness techniques, such as deep breathing or brief moments of silence, during a conversation can serve as effective tools for de-escalation. These techniques create a pause that allows individuals to collect their thoughts, regulate their emotions, and approach the discussion with a calmer and more centered demeanor.

The role of mindful communication extends beyond the resolution of immediate misunderstandings—it lays the groundwork for fostering a culture of open dialogue within relationships. Couples that embrace mindful communication as a consistent practice create an environment where ongoing misunderstandings are met with patience, empathy, and a shared commitment to mutual understanding.

Furthermore, integrating mindfulness into daily interactions can preemptively address potential sources of misunderstandings. By fostering an atmosphere of openness and attentiveness, individuals become more attuned to the needs and nuances of their partners, reducing the likelihood of misinterpretations before they escalate.

Practical strategies for expressing thoughts and emotions with clarity and empathy

Effectively expressing thoughts and emotions is an art that lies at the heart of meaningful communication. When done with clarity and empathy, it fosters understanding, connection, and nurtures the fabric of relationships. Here are practical strategies to enhance your ability to express yourself authentically, ensuring that your thoughts and emotions are communicated in a way that invites understanding and empathy.

1. Cultivate Self-Awareness: *Strategy:* Before expressing your thoughts and emotions, take a moment for self-reflection. Understand the nuances of your own feelings, the underlying reasons behind them, and how they relate to the situation. This self-awareness provides a solid foundation for clear and authentic communication.

2. Use "I" Statements: *Strategy:* Frame your expressions using "I" statements to convey your feelings and thoughts without placing blame. For example, say, "I feel..." instead of "You always..." This approach fosters a non-confrontational environment and encourages a more open dialogue.

3. Be Specific and Concrete: *Strategy:* Clearly articulate the specifics of your thoughts and emotions. Avoid vague or generalized statements. Provide concrete examples or describe the specific behavior or situation that is influencing your feelings. This precision offers your listener a clearer understanding of your perspective.

4. Active Listening: *Strategy:* Encourage a reciprocal exchange by practicing active listening. Create space for others to express themselves, and respond with genuine interest and attention. This not only establishes a respectful conversation but also sets the stage for reciprocal empathy.

5. Timing Matters: *Strategy:* Choose an appropriate time and setting for your expression. Avoid addressing sensitive topics when emotions are heightened or in the midst of other distractions. Opt for

a calm moment when both parties can engage in the conversation with focused attention.

6. **Express Emotions, Not Just Thoughts:** *Strategy:* Acknowledge and express your emotions along with your thoughts. Emotions are a natural and valid part of communication. Articulating how you feel provides a holistic view of your experience and fosters empathy from your listener.

7. **Use Non-Verbal Cues:** *Strategy:* Complement your words with non-verbal cues like facial expressions and body language. These subtle signals can enhance the emotional resonance of your message, providing additional context to your thoughts and feelings.

8. **Avoid Assumptions:** *Strategy:* Steer clear of making assumptions about what the other person knows or understands. Clearly articulate the context and background information to prevent misunderstandings. Encourage questions and seek clarification to ensure mutual understanding.

9. **Be Open to Feedback:** *Strategy:* Create an atmosphere where feedback is welcomed.

Express a willingness to hear the other person's thoughts and feelings in return. This reciprocity fosters a sense of mutual respect and contributes to a more balanced and constructive conversation.

10. Frame Criticisms Constructively: *Strategy:* If expressing criticism, frame it constructively. Focus on specific behaviors rather than making global judgments about the person. Offer suggestions for improvement and emphasize the desire for collaborative problem-solving.

11. Mindful Tone and Delivery: *Strategy:* Pay attention to your tone and delivery. A mindful approach involves speaking with intention and avoiding a confrontational or accusatory tone. A calm and measured delivery enhances the receptiveness of your message.

12. Seek Common Ground: *Strategy:* Emphasize shared goals or common ground to highlight areas of agreement. This helps create a collaborative atmosphere, fostering a sense of unity even in the midst of differing perspectives.

13. Practice Empathetic Communication: *Strategy:* Place yourself in the other person's shoes. Consider their perspective, feelings, and experiences. Acknowledge their emotions and demonstrate empathy by showing that you understand and respect their point of view.

14. Use Clear Language: *Strategy:* Choose your words carefully, opting for clear and straightforward language. Avoid jargon or overly complex expressions. Clarity in language ensures that your message is easily understood, reducing the chances of misinterpretation.

15. Offer Solutions or Next Steps: *Strategy:* If relevant, suggest potential solutions or propose actionable steps. This proactive approach demonstrates your commitment to addressing concerns collaboratively, fostering a sense of empowerment and resolution.

By incorporating these practical strategies into your communication toolkit, you empower yourself to express your thoughts and emotions with clarity and empathy. Building a foundation of effective communication not only enhances the quality of your relationships but also contributes to a culture of understanding, mutual respect, and shared growth. As you navigate the intricate terrain of human connection, these strategies serve as guiding principles, facilitating authentic and empathetic communication that strengthens the bonds you share with others.

Chapter 4: Trust and Insecurity: Nurturing Confidence in Love

The connection between overthinking, trust issues, and insecurity in relationships

Navigating the complex terrain of romantic relationships requires a delicate balance of trust, security, and open communication. However, the intricate dance between these elements can be disrupted by the pervasive presence of overthinking, giving rise to trust issues and insecurity. To understand the connection between overthinking, trust issues, and insecurity in relationships, we must delve into the ways in which the overactive mind can cast shadows over the foundations of connection.

Overthinking, characterized by a persistent and repetitive focus on thoughts, often finds fertile ground in the realm of relationships. When unchecked, it can sow seeds of doubt and uncertainty, leading individuals to scrutinize every aspect of their partner's words and actions. This hyper-analytical process can give rise to imagined scenarios, unfounded suspicions, and a heightened awareness of potential threats to the relationship.

Trust, a cornerstone of healthy relationships, is intricately connected to the ability to let go of control and embrace vulnerability. Overthinking, however, tends to foster a need for control and certainty. When the mind is consumed by a constant analysis of potential risks and uncertainties, trust can erode as individuals struggle to reconcile the perceived threats conjured by their thoughts with the reality of the relationship.

Insecurity often walks hand-in-hand with overthinking, creating a breeding ground for mistrust. The overthinker's mind, laden with self-doubt and fear, may project these insecurities onto the relationship. Whether rooted in past experiences or internalized beliefs about self-worth, insecurity becomes a lens through which the overthinker views the dynamics of the relationship, amplifying the potential for misinterpretation and suspicion.

Overthinking can manifest in various ways that contribute to the erosion of trust. Catastrophizing, a cognitive distortion where individuals envision the worst-case scenarios, becomes a common pattern. Minor disagreements or ambiguous situations may be blown out of proportion, leading to an exaggerated perception of the risks and challenges within the relationship.

Constant reassurance-seeking is another manifestation of overthinking that can strain trust. The overthinker, driven by a need for certainty and validation, may habitually seek reassurance from their partner. While reassurance is a natural part of relationships, an excessive need for it can inadvertently convey a lack of trust and contribute to a sense of suffocation within the relationship.

Moreover, overthinking often leads to a cycle of self-doubt. Individuals plagued by overthinking tendencies may question their own worthiness of love and affirmation. This self-doubt can manifest in behaviors that inadvertently undermine the foundation of trust, as the overthinker grapples with the perceived fragility of their connection.

The cycle between overthinking, trust issues, and insecurity becomes particularly challenging when left unaddressed. Trust is a dynamic element that requires a sense of security and stability to flourish. Overthinking, with its propensity to create a turbulent mental landscape, disrupts this foundation, leaving the relationship vulnerable to fractures and misunderstandings.

Open communication is a crucial antidote to the corrosive effects of overthinking on trust and insecurity. Partners must create a safe space for dialogue where fears and concerns can be shared without judgment. By openly discussing the impact of overthinking on their thoughts and emotions, individuals can foster understanding and work collaboratively to fortify the foundations of trust.

Building trust in the face of overthinking also requires a commitment to transparency. Partners can work together to establish clear expectations and boundaries. By openly communicating intentions and addressing potential triggers for overthinking, they create a roadmap for navigating challenges and uncertainties within the relationship.

Mindfulness practices play a pivotal role in breaking the cycle of overthinking and rebuilding trust. Mindfulness encourages individuals to observe their thoughts without attachment, allowing for a more balanced and realistic perspective. By cultivating mindfulness, individuals can interrupt the overthinking patterns that contribute to trust issues and insecurity.

Additionally, developing self-awareness is paramount in addressing the root causes of overthinking. Individuals must explore the sources of their insecurities and work towards building a more positive self-image. This process of self-discovery lays the groundwork for a more secure and trusting relationship with oneself and, by extension, with a partner.

Therapeutic interventions, such as couples counseling or individual therapy, can provide valuable tools for addressing overthinking, trust issues, and insecurity. A trained therapist can guide individuals and couples in developing coping mechanisms, enhancing communication skills, and fostering a deeper understanding of the dynamics at play within the relationship.

Mindfulness practices to build trust and confidence in oneself and one's partner

Embarking on a journey of building trust and confidence within oneself and a partner is a profound undertaking that requires intention, self-awareness, and a commitment to fostering a deeper connection. Mindfulness practices offer a transformative pathway toward achieving these goals, creating a space for self-discovery, open communication, and the cultivation of a resilient bond built on trust. Let's explore mindfulness practices that contribute to building trust and confidence both within oneself and within the dynamics of a relationship.

1. Self-Reflection and Awareness: Mindfulness begins with self-reflection and self-awareness. Individuals can engage in practices such as meditation or journaling to explore their thoughts, emotions, and underlying beliefs. This self-awareness lays the foundation for building trust within oneself by fostering a deeper understanding of personal values, strengths, and areas for growth.

2. Embracing the Present Moment: Mindfulness emphasizes being fully present in the current moment. Cultivating this present-moment awareness allows individuals to let go of past regrets and future anxieties that may contribute to self-doubt. By embracing the present, individuals can build confidence in their ability to navigate the challenges of the moment with clarity and resilience.

3. Non-Judgmental Self-Acceptance: Mindfulness encourages non-judgmental awareness of thoughts and feelings. This practice is transformative in fostering self-acceptance— acknowledging and embracing oneself without harsh judgment. By letting go of self-critical thoughts, individuals build trust in their own inherent worth and cultivate a more compassionate relationship with themselves.

4. Mindful Breathing for Emotional Regulation: Mindful breathing exercises are powerful tools for emotional regulation. In moments of stress or self-doubt, individuals can turn to mindful breathing to center themselves. This practice promotes a sense of calm and self-assurance, contributing to a foundation of trust in one's ability to navigate emotional landscapes.

5. Clarifying Personal Boundaries: Mindfulness involves an exploration of personal boundaries and an awareness of one's needs. Clearly defining and communicating personal boundaries builds confidence by asserting one's needs and creating a sense of safety. In a relationship, understanding and respecting each other's boundaries contribute to a trusting and secure partnership.

6. Cultivating Gratitude: Mindfulness practices often include gratitude exercises. Cultivating gratitude shifts the focus from perceived shortcomings to an appreciation of one's strengths and positive aspects of life. This practice fosters a sense of abundance and self-worth, enhancing confidence and trust in one's ability to navigate challenges.

7. Open Communication with Presence: Mindful communication involves being fully present in conversations. When expressing oneself or listening to a partner, maintaining mindful awareness fosters clear and authentic communication. This openness contributes to building trust within the relationship by creating a space where thoughts and feelings can be expressed without fear of judgment.

8. Shared Mindfulness Practices: Engaging in mindfulness practices as a couple strengthens the bond between partners. Whether through joint meditation sessions or mindful activities, shared practices create a sense of unity and connection. Building trust within the relationship becomes a collaborative effort, enhancing the confidence each partner has in the other.

9. Mindful Conflict Resolution: Mindfulness transforms the approach to conflict resolution. Instead of reacting impulsively, individuals can approach disagreements with a calm and centered mindset. This mindful approach to conflict builds trust within the relationship by creating a safe space for expressing differing opinions and working collaboratively toward resolution.

10. Compassionate Listening: Mindfulness involves cultivating deep listening skills. By practicing compassionate listening, individuals convey a genuine interest in understanding their partner's perspective. This fosters trust within the relationship, as each partner feels heard, valued, and respected.

11. Building Mindful Rituals: Establishing mindful rituals within the relationship, such as a daily check-in or gratitude practice, reinforces the connection between partners. These rituals create consistent opportunities for building trust and confidence by fostering a sense of reliability and commitment to the well-being of the relationship.

12. Mindful Appreciation: Mindfulness invites individuals to appreciate the beauty in everyday moments. Taking time to express appreciation for oneself and one's partner contributes to building confidence and trust. Acknowledging each other's strengths and efforts strengthens the foundation of the relationship.

13. Forgiveness and Letting Go: Mindfulness practices encourage the release of lingering resentments through forgiveness and letting go. By cultivating a non-judgmental attitude toward oneself and one's partner, individuals build trust by creating a space for growth, understanding, and the resolution of past conflicts.

14. Mindful Goal Setting: Setting mindful intentions and goals as individuals and as a couple provides a roadmap for personal and relational growth. Trust and confidence blossom as partners witness each other's commitment to shared aspirations and support each other's individual journeys.

15. Mindful Celebration of Achievements: Mindfulness encourages the celebration of small victories and achievements. Taking time to acknowledge and celebrate personal and shared successes fosters a positive environment. This practice builds confidence and trust within the relationship by highlighting the collective growth and resilience of the partnership.

Addressing underlying insecurities through mindful love

Navigating the intricate terrain of romantic relationships requires a nuanced understanding of the emotional landscapes that individuals bring to the union. Insecurities, often silent companions in this journey, can cast shadows over the potential for deep connection and love. Mindful love, rooted in self-awareness and compassion, provides a guiding light for addressing these underlying insecurities, fostering a relationship that thrives on authenticity, understanding, and mutual growth.

At the heart of addressing underlying insecurities through mindful love lies the practice of self-compassion. Mindfulness invites individuals to turn inward, acknowledging and embracing their vulnerabilities without judgment. By cultivating self-compassion, individuals can navigate the terrain of their insecurities with kindness, recognizing that imperfections are a natural part of the human experience.

Mindful love involves an exploration of the origins of insecurities, delving into the depths of past experiences, traumas, or societal influences that may have contributed to the development of these internal narratives. By shining a light on the roots of insecurities, individuals can gain a clearer understanding of the patterns that may be influencing their thoughts and behaviors within the relationship.

Open communication is a cornerstone of mindful love, providing a space where individuals can share their insecurities with vulnerability and without fear of judgment. Expressing one's inner struggles requires a level of trust that mindful love seeks to nurture. Partners can engage in open and honest conversations, creating an atmosphere where insecurities are met with empathy and mutual understanding.

Mindful love also involves actively listening to a partner's expressions of insecurity. Rather than dismissing or attempting to "fix" these feelings, mindful listening entails a deep and empathetic engagement. Partners can create a safe space for each other to share their insecurities, knowing that they will be met with compassion and acceptance.

The cultivation of mindfulness within a relationship encourages partners to be present with each other in moments of vulnerability. This presence involves a conscious effort to set aside distractions and fully engage with a partner's emotions, creating a profound connection that transcends the surface of insecurities. Through mindful presence, individuals reassure each other that they are seen and valued, fostering a sense of security within the relationship.

Mindful love encourages partners to co-create a narrative of shared values and intentions. By collaboratively establishing a foundation built on trust, respect, and mutual support, couples can actively work towards dispelling the shadows of insecurity. This shared narrative becomes a guiding force, shaping the relationship in a way that honors the unique vulnerabilities and strengths each partner brings to the union.

The practice of mindfulness also involves acknowledging the impermanence of thoughts and emotions. Insecurities, like passing clouds, can be observed without attachment. By adopting a non-judgmental attitude towards insecurities, individuals can free themselves from the grip of negative self-talk and create space for self-growth and acceptance.

Mindful love calls for a commitment to personal growth and development. Partners embark on a journey of self-discovery, acknowledging that their individual paths contribute to the richness of the relationship. By fostering a culture of continuous growth, mindful love creates an environment where insecurities are not perceived as limitations but as opportunities for learning and evolution.

Couples practicing mindful love may find solace in shared mindfulness activities. Whether engaging in meditation, mindful walks, or other contemplative practices, these activities provide opportunities for partners to connect on a deeper level. Mindful experiences become a shared language, reinforcing the bond between partners and creating a reservoir of resilience in the face of insecurities.

Moreover, the practice of gratitude within mindful love becomes a powerful antidote to insecurities. Partners can intentionally focus on and appreciate each other's positive qualities, fostering a sense of abundance and acknowledgment. Expressing gratitude becomes

a ritual that fortifies the emotional foundation of
the relationship.

Chapter 5: Breaking the Cycle of Negative Thoughts: A Mindful Approach

Explore the cycle of negative thoughts associated with overthinking

Embarking on an exploration of the intricate cycle of negative thoughts associated with overthinking unveils the complex interplay between the mind and emotions. Overthinking, often insidious in its nature, can give rise to a relentless cycle of destructive thoughts that permeate various aspects of one's life. Understanding this cycle involves delving into the origins, patterns, and consequences of these negative thoughts, shedding light on the mental landscape that overthinking creates.

At the core of the overthinking cycle lies a web of incessant rumination. The mind, driven by a relentless need to analyze, replay, and dissect every aspect of a situation, becomes entangled in a never-ending loop of thought. This loop often begins with a trigger—a perceived threat, an unresolved issue, or an ambiguous situation. The trigger serves as the catalyst for the mind to plunge into a spiral of overanalysis.

As the overthinking cycle gains momentum, negative thoughts start to take root. These thoughts, often fueled by fear, self-doubt, or anxiety, begin to shape the narrative of the mind.

Individuals may find themselves dwelling on worst-case scenarios, imagining potential pitfalls, or engaging in catastrophic thinking that magnifies the perceived risks associated with a situation.

Negative thoughts within the overthinking cycle are not static; they evolve and multiply. One negative thought begets another, creating a chain reaction that intensifies the emotional impact. The mind, now a battleground of conflicting thoughts, amplifies the emotional toll of the original trigger, contributing to heightened stress, worry, and a sense of helplessness.

The overthinking cycle is further exacerbated by the tendency to engage in self-criticism. Negative thoughts often turn inward, leading individuals to question their own abilities, decisions, or worthiness. This self-critical stance becomes a reinforcing mechanism, deepening the overthinking cycle as individuals internalize and personalize the negative narrative that overthinking creates.

Moreover, the overthinking cycle is characterized by a skewed perception of control. Overthinkers, driven by a need for certainty and security, believe that by continuously analyzing a situation, they can somehow gain control over its outcome. This illusory sense of control becomes a driving force in the overthinking cycle, compelling individuals to persist in their mental gymnastics despite the diminishing returns on their efforts.

The negative thoughts associated with overthinking often spill over into various aspects of life. Relationships may bear the brunt of distorted perceptions, as overthinkers project their anxieties onto interactions with others. Work and personal goals may become overshadowed by a pervasive sense of inadequacy, hindering productivity and stifling personal growth.

The consequences of the overthinking cycle extend beyond the realm of mental and emotional well-being. The physical toll of chronic overthinking can manifest in symptoms such as fatigue, tension, and even disrupted sleep patterns. The mind-body connection becomes evident as negative thoughts contribute to a heightened state of physiological arousal, perpetuating a cycle of stress and unease.

Breaking free from the overthinking cycle requires a conscious effort to interrupt its patterns. Mindfulness, with its emphasis on present-moment awareness, becomes a powerful ally in this endeavor. By cultivating mindfulness, individuals can observe their thoughts without becoming entangled in them. This non-judgmental observation creates a space for detachment from the negative thoughts, allowing individuals to gain a more balanced and objective perspective.

Mindfulness practices, such as meditation and deep breathing, serve as anchors in the tumultuous sea of overthinking. These practices provide a refuge, a momentary reprieve from the cycle of negative thoughts. Through intentional focus on the breath or a present-moment anchor, individuals can quiet the mental chatter and create a sense of calm within the storm of overthinking.

Another key aspect of breaking the overthinking cycle involves challenging negative thoughts through cognitive restructuring. This process entails examining the validity of negative thoughts, identifying cognitive distortions, and reframing the narrative. By actively questioning the accuracy of negative thoughts, individuals can begin to unravel the automatic patterns that fuel the overthinking cycle.

Therapeutic interventions, such as cognitive-behavioral therapy (CBT), offer structured frameworks for addressing the overthinking cycle. CBT equips individuals with tools to identify and challenge negative thoughts, replacing them with more balanced and realistic perspectives. The therapeutic process becomes a collaborative journey toward breaking free from the shackles of overthinking.

Techniques for breaking the pattern of negative thinking

Breaking the pattern of negative thinking is a transformative journey that involves a conscious and intentional effort to shift mental habits and cultivate a more positive mindset. The cycle of negative thoughts can be pervasive, affecting various aspects of life and well-being. To break free from this pattern, individuals can explore a range of techniques that empower them to challenge and reshape their thought patterns.

One fundamental technique for breaking the pattern of negative thinking is mindfulness. Mindfulness involves cultivating present-moment awareness without judgment. By paying attention to thoughts as they arise, individuals can create a mental space that allows them to observe negative thoughts without becoming entangled in them. Mindfulness techniques, such as mindful breathing and meditation, provide practical tools to anchor the mind in the present, disrupting the automatic cycle of negative thinking.

Cognitive restructuring is another powerful technique that involves actively challenging and reframing negative thoughts. This process requires individuals to identify cognitive distortions—patterns of thought that contribute to negativity—and replace them with more balanced and realistic perspectives. By consciously questioning the accuracy of negative thoughts, individuals can interrupt the automatic patterns that fuel the cycle of negativity.

Affirmations serve as a proactive technique to counteract negative thinking. Affirmations are positive statements that individuals repeat to themselves, focusing on cultivating a positive mindset. By consistently affirming positive beliefs about oneself and the world, individuals can gradually shift their thought patterns and foster a more optimistic outlook.

Gratitude practices offer a transformative approach to breaking the cycle of negative thinking. Engaging in regular gratitude exercises involves reflecting on and expressing gratitude for positive aspects of one's life. This practice shifts the focus from what is lacking to what is present, fostering a sense of abundance and countering the habitual pull of negative thoughts.

Behavioral activation is a technique that involves engaging in activities that bring a sense of pleasure or accomplishment. Breaking the pattern of negative thinking often requires interrupting the inertia of inactivity that negativity can perpetuate. By consciously participating in enjoyable or meaningful activities, individuals can create positive experiences that counteract the impact of negative thoughts.

The technique of thought stopping involves consciously interrupting negative thoughts when they arise. This technique requires individuals to mentally say "stop" when they notice a negative thought taking hold. The goal is to create a moment of pause, allowing individuals to redirect their attention and choose a more constructive thought pattern.

Journaling is a reflective technique that can help individuals gain insights into their negative thought patterns. Keeping a journal allows individuals to record their thoughts and emotions, identifying recurring themes and triggers. By gaining a deeper understanding of the patterns at play, individuals can take proactive steps to challenge and reframe negative thoughts.

Setting realistic and achievable goals is a technique that empowers individuals to focus on positive outcomes. By breaking down larger goals into smaller, manageable steps, individuals create a sense of accomplishment and build confidence. This process counteracts the negative thinking pattern that often emerges when faced with overwhelming or unattainable goals.

Mindful self-compassion involves treating oneself with kindness and understanding, especially in the face of negative thoughts. This technique encourages individuals to approach themselves with the same compassion they would offer to a friend facing challenges. By cultivating self-compassion, individuals can break the cycle of harsh self-judgment that often accompanies negative thinking.

The practice of visualization is a technique that involves creating mental images of positive outcomes. By vividly imagining success, happiness, or desired outcomes, individuals can reshape their mental landscape. Visualization serves as a powerful tool for interrupting the pattern of negative thinking and fostering a more optimistic and constructive mindset.

Social connection is a technique that leverages the power of relationships to break the cycle of negative thinking. Engaging in meaningful conversations, seeking support from friends or loved ones, and participating in social activities create opportunities for positive interactions. Social connection serves as a buffer against isolation and reinforces a sense of belonging, countering the impact of negative thoughts.

Mindful movement, such as yoga or tai chi, is a technique that integrates physical activity with mindfulness. Engaging in mindful movement practices not only promotes physical well-being but also helps individuals connect with the present moment. This integration of movement and mindfulness serves as a holistic approach to breaking the pattern of negative thinking.

Mindfulness exercises for challenging and reframing negative thoughts in relationships

In relationships, the ability to navigate and reframe negative thoughts is essential for fostering understanding, empathy, and mutual growth. Mindfulness exercises serve as valuable tools to cultivate awareness and break the automatic patterns of negative thinking that can arise within the dynamics of a relationship. These exercises encourage individuals to approach their thoughts with a non-judgmental mindset, promoting a more balanced and constructive perspective.

One effective mindfulness exercise for challenging negative thoughts in relationships is the "Observing Thoughts" technique. In this exercise, individuals take on the role of an observer of their thoughts. Instead of immediately reacting to negative thoughts, they step back mentally and observe them without attachment. This practice creates a space for individuals to gain perspective on their thought patterns, allowing for a more intentional and measured response to negative thoughts within the relationship.

The "Mindful Breathing" exercise is a foundational mindfulness practice that can be particularly powerful in challenging negative thoughts. By focusing on the breath and bringing attention to each inhale and exhale, individuals ground themselves in the present moment. This exercise helps break the cycle of rumination and allows for a mental reset, providing clarity and calmness when confronted with negative thoughts in the context of a relationship.

Another mindfulness exercise for reframing negative thoughts in relationships involves cultivating a "Gratitude Journal." Participants take a few moments each day to reflect on and jot down aspects of their relationship for which they are grateful. This practice shifts the focus from negativity to positive aspects, fostering a mindset of appreciation and helping individuals reframe their thoughts to acknowledge the strengths and joys within the relationship.

The "Five Senses Grounding" exercise is a mindfulness technique that encourages individuals to engage their senses fully in the present moment. When negative thoughts arise in a relationship, individuals can ground themselves by focusing on what they see, hear, touch, taste, and smell in the current environment. This sensory awareness helps redirect attention away from negative thoughts and promotes a sense of presence and connection within the relationship.

"Mindful Reflection" is an exercise that involves setting aside dedicated time for self-reflection on one's thoughts and emotions in the context of the relationship. Individuals create a quiet space for introspection, allowing them to explore the root causes of negative thoughts and gain insights into their triggers. This mindfulness exercise promotes self-awareness and a deeper understanding of the thought patterns influencing the relationship.

A guided mindfulness meditation for relationships can be a transformative practice for challenging negative thoughts. In this exercise, individuals listen to a guided meditation that specifically addresses negative thoughts within the context of relationships. The meditation may include prompts for self-reflection, cultivating compassion, and reframing thoughts to foster a more positive and constructive mindset.

The "Loving-Kindness Meditation" is a mindfulness exercise that focuses on generating feelings of love and compassion, not only for oneself but also for others, including one's partner. By extending wishes for well-being and happiness to both oneself and the partner, individuals cultivate a mindset of kindness that counteracts negative thoughts and promotes a more loving and supportive dynamic in the relationship.

Mindful communication exercises can be instrumental in addressing negative thoughts within the context of relationships. These exercises involve conscious and attentive listening, where individuals fully engage in the present moment during conversations with their partners. Mindful communication encourages an open and non-judgmental exchange of thoughts and feelings, creating an environment where negative thoughts can be expressed and reframed collaboratively.

The "Body Scan" mindfulness exercise is a technique that involves systematically bringing awareness to different parts of the body. When negative thoughts arise in relationships, individuals can use the body scan to ground themselves in bodily sensations, promoting a sense of presence and detachment from the thoughts. This exercise contributes to a more embodied and centered experience within the relationship.

Incorporating a "Digital Detox" mindfulness practice can be beneficial for challenging negative thoughts in relationships, especially in the age of constant connectivity. This exercise involves intentionally taking breaks from digital devices to create moments of mindfulness and connection with one's partner. By reducing digital distractions, individuals can foster a more authentic and present connection, diminishing the space for negative thoughts to thrive.

Chapter 6: Mindful Conflict Resolution: Turning Tensions into Opportunities

Role of overthinking in conflicts within relationships

Overthinking, a subtle but potent force, can cast a shadow over the landscape of relationships, often playing a pivotal role in conflicts that arise between partners. The intricate interplay between thoughts, emotions, and interpretations within the realm of overthinking can magnify disagreements, create misunderstandings, and contribute to the escalation of conflicts. Understanding the role of overthinking in relationship conflicts requires delving into the ways it manifests, influences communication dynamics, and contributes to the perpetuation of discord.

At its core, overthinking involves an excessive and repetitive focus on thoughts, often driven by a need for control or a desire to predict and prevent potential issues. In the context of relationships, overthinking can become a silent companion during moments of disagreement or tension. Instead of addressing issues directly, individuals may find themselves caught in a web of thoughts, analyzing past events, anticipating future scenarios, and creating intricate mental narratives that may not align with the reality of the situation.

One prominent way overthinking contributes to conflicts is through the lens of catastrophizing. Overthinkers, fueled by a heightened sensitivity to potential threats, may engage in catastrophic thinking, envisioning the worst possible outcomes of a disagreement or conflict. This distorted perception can intensify emotions, making a relatively minor issue appear insurmountable and exacerbating the conflict.

Overthinking also tends to fuel the cycle of misinterpretation. As individuals become entangled in their own thoughts, they may misread cues, assign incorrect motivations to their partner's actions, or assume negative intentions where none exist. This misalignment between perceived reality and actual intentions can give rise to misunderstandings, creating a fertile ground for conflicts to take root and flourish.

In the midst of conflicts, overthinking often manifests in the form of replaying conversations or events. Individuals may obsessively revisit arguments, analyzing every word spoken and every nuance of body language. This continual replaying can deepen emotional wounds, intensify negative emotions, and hinder the resolution process by keeping the focus on past grievances rather than constructive solutions.

Moreover, overthinking can contribute to a breakdown in communication during conflicts. When individuals are consumed by their own thoughts, active listening may be compromised, and the ability to empathize with a partner's perspective can be overshadowed. Overthinkers may become so preoccupied with their internal dialogue that they struggle to engage in the present moment, hindering the potential for effective communication and conflict resolution.

The role of overthinking in conflicts extends to the realm of assumptions and projections. Overthinkers, grappling with their internal dialogue, may project their fears, insecurities, or past experiences onto their partners. These projections can create a distorted narrative, where conflicts become not only about the present disagreement but also about unresolved issues from the past or anxieties about the future.

In the heat of conflicts, overthinking may lead to a heightened state of defensiveness. Individuals driven by overthinking tendencies may feel the need to protect themselves from perceived threats, leading to an instinctive reaction of self-preservation. This defensiveness can further escalate conflicts, as partners may interpret it as a lack of openness or receptivity to resolving issues collaboratively.

The perpetual nature of overthinking can contribute to a cycle of conflict avoidance. Fearful of the potential consequences of addressing conflicts directly, overthinkers may retreat into their thoughts, avoiding necessary conversations and delaying the resolution process. This avoidance, while providing temporary relief, can lead to a buildup of unresolved issues that may resurface later, potentially causing more significant conflicts.

Breaking free from the grip of overthinking in the context of relationship conflicts requires a conscious effort to cultivate mindfulness. Mindfulness encourages individuals to observe their thoughts without attachment, creating a space for more intentional responses to conflicts. By bringing attention to the present moment, individuals can interrupt the overthinking cycle and engage in conflicts with greater clarity and presence.

Communication skills play a pivotal role in mitigating the impact of overthinking on conflicts. Partners can work together to create an open and non-judgmental space for expressing thoughts and emotions. By fostering an environment where both individuals feel heard and valued, conflicts can be approached with a sense of collaboration rather than adversarial thinking.

Setting clear communication expectations and boundaries becomes crucial in addressing overthinking within conflicts. Establishing guidelines for how conflicts will be approached, such as using "I" statements, actively listening, and taking breaks when needed, creates a structured framework that helps mitigate the influence of overthinking on communication dynamics.

Therapeutic interventions, such as couples counseling, can offer valuable support in breaking the cycle of overthinking within relationship conflicts. A trained therapist can guide partners in developing effective communication strategies, exploring the roots of overthinking tendencies, and providing tools for managing conflicts in a healthier and more constructive manner.

A mindful approach to conflict resolution, emphasizing understanding and empathy

Approaching conflict resolution through a mindful lens introduces a transformative paradigm that transcends traditional approaches, placing emphasis on understanding, empathy, and the cultivation of a harmonious connection between individuals. Mindfulness, rooted in the present moment and non-judgmental awareness, offers a unique framework for navigating conflicts with a sense of clarity, compassion, and a commitment to mutual understanding.

At the heart of a mindful approach to conflict resolution lies the concept of present-moment awareness. Instead of allowing the mind to dwell on past grievances or anxieties about the future, individuals practicing mindfulness bring their attention to the current situation. This intentional focus on the present allows for a more grounded and objective perspective, enabling individuals to engage in conflict resolution with a clear and open mindset.

Central to the mindful approach is the cultivation of understanding. In conflict situations, misunderstandings often arise from differing perspectives, assumptions, or misinterpretations. Mindfulness encourages individuals to suspend judgment and actively listen to each other, seeking to understand the underlying emotions, needs, and concerns that contribute to the conflict. This empathetic listening fosters a deeper connection and lays the foundation for a more meaningful resolution.

Empathy, a cornerstone of the mindful approach to conflict resolution, involves the ability to vicariously experience and understand another person's feelings. By cultivating empathy, individuals step into the shoes of their partners, acknowledging and validating their emotions. This empathetic connection forms a bridge between conflicting perspectives, creating a space for mutual recognition and a shared commitment to finding common ground.

Mindfulness also encourages individuals to observe their own reactions and responses during conflicts. Instead of reacting impulsively based on habitual patterns or past conditioning, individuals practicing mindfulness pause to reflect on their own emotions and triggers. This self-awareness allows for a more intentional and measured response, reducing the likelihood of escalating the conflict and creating an opening for constructive dialogue.

The concept of non-judgmental awareness is fundamental to the mindful approach. In conflict resolution, individuals often carry judgments about themselves or their partners, contributing to an adversarial dynamic. Mindfulness invites a non-judgmental stance, where individuals observe their thoughts and emotions without attaching value judgments. This shift in perspective fosters an environment of acceptance and openness, creating space for resolution without blame or criticism.

A key element of mindfulness in conflict resolution involves the practice of deep listening. Deep listening goes beyond hearing words; it involves fully immersing oneself in the speaker's experience, both verbal and non-verbal. This practice requires undivided attention, putting aside preconceived notions and actively engaging in the moment. Deep listening allows individuals to absorb the nuances of their partner's communication, promoting a more thorough understanding and paving the way for effective resolution.

Mindful breathing serves as a grounding technique in conflict resolution. When emotions run high, individuals can turn to mindful breathing to center themselves. By focusing on the breath, individuals create a moment of pause, allowing them to respond to the conflict from a place of calmness and clarity. Mindful breathing serves as an anchor in the turbulent waters of conflict, facilitating a more composed and thoughtful engagement.

The mindful approach to conflict resolution encourages individuals to embrace a curious and exploratory mindset. Instead of approaching conflicts with a fixed agenda or a desire to "win," individuals practicing mindfulness adopt a curious stance, seeking to understand the underlying dynamics and motivations. This curiosity opens the door to collaborative problem-solving, where both parties contribute to finding creative and mutually beneficial solutions.

Mindful communication techniques play a vital role in conflict resolution. The use of "I" statements, expressing thoughts and feelings without blame, and using language that promotes understanding and connection are hallmarks of mindful communication. By choosing words mindfully and with care, individuals can foster an atmosphere of respect and cooperation, even in the midst of conflict.

Mindful conflict resolution also involves the intentional cultivation of positive emotions. Amidst the challenges of conflict, individuals can intentionally bring attention to positive aspects of the relationship, past positive experiences, or shared values. This focus on positivity counteracts the gravitational pull of negativity and contributes to a more optimistic and solution-oriented mindset.

An important aspect of the mindful approach is the concept of forgiveness. Instead of holding onto resentment or grievances, individuals practicing mindfulness understand the liberating power of forgiveness. Forgiveness does not mean condoning harmful behavior, but rather, it involves letting go of the emotional baggage that may impede the resolution process. By embracing forgiveness, individuals create space for healing and renewal within the relationship.

Practical steps and exercises for resolving conflicts mindfully

Navigating conflicts mindfully involves a deliberate and conscious approach to resolution that prioritizes understanding, empathy, and collaborative problem-solving. Practical steps and exercises can serve as valuable tools in cultivating a mindful approach to conflict resolution, fostering an environment where conflicts become opportunities for growth, connection, and mutual understanding.

One practical step in resolving conflicts mindfully is to initiate the process with a calm and centered mindset. Before engaging in discussions, take a moment to practice mindful breathing. Close your eyes, focus on your breath, and allow yourself to be present in the moment. This mindful breathing exercise creates a foundation of composure and clarity, enabling you to approach the conflict with a more open and receptive mindset.

Active listening is a cornerstone of mindful conflict resolution. During discussions, make a conscious effort to truly listen to your partner. Avoid interrupting and resist the urge to formulate your response while the other person is speaking. Instead, practice deep listening by giving your full attention, making eye contact, and acknowledging what is being said. This fosters an atmosphere of respect and creates a space for authentic communication.

Mindful communication involves expressing yourself with clarity and intention. Use "I" statements to convey your thoughts and feelings without placing blame on the other person. For example, instead of saying, "You always do this," say, "I feel upset when this happens." This shift in language promotes personal responsibility and encourages a collaborative dialogue rather than a confrontational exchange.

The "Three Breaths Pause" is a practical exercise that can be employed during conflicts. When tensions rise, take three intentional breaths before responding. This brief pause allows you to step back from reactive emotions and approach the conflict with a more measured and thoughtful response. The Three Breaths Pause serves as a valuable tool for preventing impulsive reactions and promoting mindful engagement.

Mindful reflection is a proactive step in conflict resolution. Take time to reflect on your own emotions, needs, and triggers before engaging in discussions. Journaling can be a helpful exercise in this regard. Write down your thoughts and feelings, exploring the underlying causes of the conflict from your perspective. This self-awareness contributes to a more mindful and intentional approach to resolution.

The "Five Why's" technique is a mindful inquiry exercise that delves into the root causes of conflicts. Ask yourself why the conflict occurred, and then continue asking "why" to each subsequent response. This iterative process helps uncover deeper layers of understanding, revealing the underlying issues that may not be immediately apparent. The Five Why's technique encourages a more nuanced and comprehensive exploration of the conflict.

Cultivating empathy is a vital step in mindful conflict resolution. The "Compassionate Listening" exercise involves actively putting yourself in your partner's shoes. Seek to understand their perspective, emotions, and needs without judgment. This practice of compassionate listening fosters empathy, creating a bridge between differing viewpoints and laying the groundwork for collaborative resolution.

The "Reflective Mirroring" exercise is a practical tool for ensuring that both parties feel heard and understood. After one person expresses their thoughts or feelings, the other person reflects back what they heard. This reflective mirroring allows for clarification and validation, reducing the likelihood of misinterpretations and creating a shared understanding of the issues at hand.

Visualization techniques can also be employed in mindful conflict resolution. Before engaging in discussions, take a moment to visualize a positive and constructive resolution to the conflict. Picture both parties expressing themselves with clarity, understanding each other's perspectives, and collaboratively working towards a solution. Visualization creates a positive mental framework, influencing the actual interaction in a mindful and constructive direction.

Mindful decision-making is integral to resolving conflicts effectively. Instead of focusing on winning or losing, approach decisions collaboratively. The "Pros and Cons" exercise involves jointly listing the potential advantages and disadvantages of different solutions. This collaborative exploration fosters a sense of shared responsibility and empowers both parties to contribute to the decision-making process.

The "Gratitude Exchange" is a mindful exercise that shifts the focus from conflict to appreciation. Take turns expressing gratitude for positive aspects of the relationship. This exercise creates a positive atmosphere, reminding both parties of the strengths and joys within the relationship. Engaging in a gratitude exchange fosters a mindset of appreciation and can contribute to a more amicable resolution.

Silence can be a powerful ally in mindful conflict resolution. The "Silent Reflection" exercise involves taking a few moments of intentional silence during discussions. This silence allows both parties to reflect on what has been said, fostering a deeper understanding and creating space for more thoughtful responses. Silent reflection promotes a mindful and contemplative atmosphere.

Setting intentions for the resolution process is a practical step that aligns with mindfulness. Before entering into discussions, set positive and constructive intentions for the outcome. This may involve expressing a desire for mutual understanding, a commitment to finding common ground, or a focus on collaborative problem-solving. Setting intentions establishes a mindful framework that guides the resolution process.

Chapter 7: Balancing Independence and Togetherness: Mindful Interdependence

How overthinking can impact the balance between independence and togetherness

The intricate dance between independence and togetherness is a delicate equilibrium that defines the dynamics of relationships. Overthinking, with its penchant for relentless analysis and anticipation, can significantly impact this balance, introducing challenges that reverberate through the intricacies of personal autonomy and shared connection.

At its core, overthinking can lead to an overemphasis on independence, fueling a sense of self-sufficiency that borders on isolation. Individuals prone to overthinking may find themselves immersed in a mental landscape where self-reliance becomes a coping mechanism. The constant analysis of situations, decisions, and potential outcomes can create a hesitancy to rely on others or share vulnerabilities, leading to a fortress of independence that hinders the natural flow of connection in relationships.

Conversely, overthinking can also tip the scales toward an excessive desire for togetherness. The mind, driven by a relentless need for reassurance and certainty, may envision potential threats to the relationship. This fear of separation can manifest in a clinginess or an overreliance on the partner for emotional validation and support. Overthinkers may struggle to navigate the fine line between interdependence and unhealthy dependency, impacting the natural rhythm of togetherness within the relationship.

Overthinking can breed uncertainty, and this uncertainty often extends to the realm of personal boundaries. Individuals grappling with overthinking tendencies may find themselves constantly analyzing the boundaries between themselves and their partners. The fear of encroachment on personal space or the anxiety about being too distant can lead to a perpetual state of questioning and recalibrating, disrupting the fluidity of the balance between independence and togetherness.

Furthermore, the impact of overthinking on communication can influence the delicate equilibrium between independence and togetherness. Overthinkers may hesitate to express their needs or desires, fearing that asserting themselves will upset the delicate balance within the relationship. Alternatively, the constant analysis of communication nuances can lead to misinterpretations, creating unnecessary tensions that disrupt the harmonious flow between independence and togetherness.

Overthinking often intertwines with insecurity, a potent force that can tip the scales in either direction. Insecurity may lead to an exaggerated need for independence as a defense mechanism against potential rejection or disappointment. On the other hand, it can foster an intense desire for constant togetherness as a means of seeking validation and reassurance. The nuanced interplay between overthinking and insecurity further complicates the delicate dance between autonomy and connection in relationships.

The impact of overthinking on decision-making can also influence the balance between independence and togetherness. Overthinkers may grapple with even the simplest choices, fearing the consequences of their decisions on the relationship. This hesitation can hinder personal autonomy, creating a reliance on the partner's input or approval. Conversely, the constant need for reassurance may lead to decision-making based solely on the desire for togetherness, compromising individual autonomy.

The constant mental chatter of overthinking can create an internal barrier to vulnerability. The fear of judgment or rejection may prevent individuals from openly expressing their emotions or seeking support when needed. This hesitancy to be vulnerable can impact the emotional intimacy that underpins the togetherness aspect of a relationship, hindering the natural ebb and flow between independence and shared connection.

The impact of overthinking on the balance between independence and togetherness becomes particularly pronounced during times of stress or uncertainty. Overthinkers may instinctively retreat into their minds, intensifying the quest for self-reliance or amplifying the desire for constant togetherness as a source of comfort. This heightened reactivity can disrupt the natural equilibrium, making it challenging for the relationship to navigate challenges with flexibility and resilience.

Breaking free from the clutches of overthinking requires a conscious effort to cultivate mindfulness and self-awareness. By bringing attention to the present moment, individuals can observe their thoughts without becoming entangled in them. This non-judgmental awareness creates a space for intentional choices, allowing individuals to navigate the balance between independence and togetherness with greater clarity and authenticity.

Effective communication plays a pivotal role in restoring balance. Open and honest conversations about individual needs, boundaries, and expectations create a shared understanding within the relationship. Setting clear communication expectations allows both partners to express their desires for independence and togetherness without fear of misinterpretation, fostering a more harmonious connection.

Establishing healthy boundaries is crucial in navigating the impact of overthinking on the balance between independence and togetherness. This involves a collaborative effort to define personal space, autonomy, and shared activities within the relationship. By proactively discussing and respecting each other's boundaries, partners can create a supportive environment that encourages both independence and togetherness.

Couples counseling can be a valuable resource for navigating the challenges posed by overthinking in relationships. A trained therapist can guide partners in exploring the impact of overthinking, fostering effective communication, and developing strategies for maintaining a healthy balance between independence and togetherness. The therapeutic process becomes a collaborative journey toward resilience and mutual understanding.

Discuss the concept of mindful interdependence in relationships

The concept of mindful interdependence in relationships represents a nuanced and intentional approach to connection that goes beyond traditional notions of independence and togetherness. Rooted in the principles of mindfulness, this perspective encourages a harmonious interplay between individual autonomy and shared connection, fostering a dynamic and resilient foundation for relationships to thrive.

Mindful interdependence begins with a conscious recognition of each individual as a unique and autonomous being. Rather than viewing independence and togetherness as opposing forces, mindful interdependence embraces the idea that individuals can maintain their individuality while actively contributing to the shared connection. This recognition forms the cornerstone of a relationship where each partner is valued for their distinct qualities, experiences, and perspectives.

At the heart of mindful interdependence lies a commitment to self-awareness. Individuals engaged in mindful interdependence continually cultivate an understanding of their own needs, desires, and boundaries. This self-awareness serves as a compass for navigating the complexities of relationships, allowing individuals to engage with authenticity and communicate their needs effectively within the context of the partnership.

Mindful interdependence invites individuals to approach relationships with a sense of present-moment awareness. The practice of mindfulness encourages individuals to be fully engaged in the current experience, free from the burdens of past grievances or anxieties about the future. This presence in the moment fosters a deeper connection between partners, allowing for a more authentic and responsive interaction that transcends preconceived notions or habitual reactions.

Communication in mindful interdependence is characterized by open dialogue, active listening, and non-judgmental understanding. Partners engage in conversations that go beyond surface-level interactions, exploring the depths of each other's thoughts, feelings, and aspirations. The emphasis on empathetic listening creates a supportive environment where both individuals feel heard, valued, and respected, contributing to a more profound sense of connection.

A key aspect of mindful interdependence is the recognition of interbeing—the understanding that individuals are interconnected and their well-being is intertwined. This concept transcends the boundaries of ego-centric thinking and emphasizes the collective nature of the relationship. Partners in a mindful interdependent relationship recognize that their actions, choices, and emotions have ripple effects on the overall dynamic, fostering a sense of shared responsibility and mutual influence.

Mindful interdependence also involves the cultivation of emotional intelligence. Partners actively work to understand and regulate their own emotions while also being attuned to the emotional experiences of their significant other. This heightened emotional awareness contributes to a more empathetic and supportive connection, creating space for shared emotional growth within the relationship.

The concept of shared goals and values is integral to mindful interdependence. While each individual maintains their autonomy, there is a deliberate effort to align on common aspirations and principles. This shared sense of purpose serves as a unifying force, providing a roadmap for the relationship's growth and development while honoring the individuality of each partner.

In mindful interdependence, the ebb and flow of the relationship are acknowledged and embraced. Partners recognize that relationships, like life itself, are dynamic and subject to change. Rather than resisting inevitable shifts, mindful interdependence encourages adaptability and resilience. This acceptance of change fosters an environment where the relationship can evolve organically, allowing both partners to navigate the journey together with a sense of equanimity.

Conflict resolution within mindful interdependence is approached with a spirit of collaboration and mutual understanding. Conflicts are viewed as opportunities for growth and learning rather than threats to the relationship. Partners engage in open and constructive conversations, exploring solutions that honor both individual needs and the well-being of the relationship as a whole. Mindful conflict resolution involves a commitment to listening, learning, and co-creating resolutions that contribute to the ongoing flourishing of the partnership.

Mindful interdependence is not a static state but an ongoing practice that requires intention and commitment. It involves a continuous exploration of the balance between autonomy and connection, a commitment to self-awareness, and an openness to the evolving nature of the relationship. Partners in a mindful interdependent relationship actively participate in their own growth and the growth of the partnership, creating a dynamic and fulfilling shared journey.

Insights and exercises for cultivating a healthy balance in love

Cultivating a healthy balance in love is an intricate and ongoing journey that requires self-awareness, intentionality, and a commitment to the well-being of both individuals in the relationship. Insights and exercises play a crucial role in this process, offering valuable tools for partners to navigate the complexities of love with authenticity, harmony, and mutual growth.

Insight 1: **Embrace Individuality within Unity** A healthy balance in love begins with the recognition and celebration of individuality within the context of unity. Each partner brings a unique set of qualities, perspectives, and aspirations to the relationship. Embracing and honoring these individual differences fosters an environment where both individuals feel valued and acknowledged. Exercise: Take time for personal reflections and share insights about your individual values, goals, and preferences with your partner. This exercise encourages open communication and strengthens the foundation of understanding within the relationship.

Insight 2: **Cultivate Open and Honest Communication** Effective communication is the cornerstone of a healthy love balance. Encourage a culture of openness, where both partners feel safe expressing their thoughts, feelings, and needs without fear of judgment. Honest communication builds trust and intimacy, creating a solid framework for a balanced and thriving relationship. Exercise: Practice active listening by dedicating specific moments to fully engage with your partner's thoughts and feelings. Reflect back what you hear to ensure mutual understanding, fostering a deeper connection through meaningful communication.

Insight 3: **Prioritize Self-Care for Mutual Well-Being** A healthy balance in love involves recognizing the importance of individual well-being. Partners must prioritize self-care to maintain a strong foundation for the relationship. This includes attending to physical, emotional, and mental health needs. Exercise: Collaborate on creating a shared self-care routine that integrates individual practices. This could include setting aside time for personal hobbies, exercise, or relaxation. Mutual support for each other's self-care contributes to a balanced and resilient partnership.

Insight 4: **Navigate Conflict with Compassion** Conflict is inevitable in any relationship, but how it is navigated can significantly impact the balance of love. Cultivate a mindset of compassion and understanding during disagreements. Avoid blame and instead focus on collaborative problem-solving. Exercise: Develop a conflict resolution plan together. Identify triggers, establish communication guidelines, and agree on a process for resolving conflicts. This exercise empowers partners to approach conflicts with empathy and a shared commitment to finding constructive solutions.

Insight 5: **Foster Shared Dreams and Goals** A healthy love balance involves aligning on shared dreams and goals for the future. This shared vision provides a sense of purpose and direction, strengthening the bond between partners. Exercise: Set aside time to discuss your individual aspirations and identify areas of overlap. Collaboratively create a vision board or a written plan that outlines shared goals, fostering a sense of unity and mutual investment in the relationship's growth.

Insight 6: **Celebrate Small Moments of Connection** In the pursuit of a healthy love balance, it's essential to appreciate and celebrate the small moments of connection in everyday life. These moments contribute to a sense of shared joy and intimacy. Exercise: Establish a daily or weekly ritual that promotes connection, such as sharing a meal, taking a walk together, or expressing gratitude for each other. Consistent acknowledgment of these small moments fosters a positive atmosphere within the relationship.

Insight 7: **Embrace Flexibility and Adaptability** A healthy love balance involves an inherent flexibility and adaptability to the ever-changing nature of life. Circumstances, priorities, and individuals evolve over time, requiring partners to navigate these changes together. Exercise: Engage in joint decision-making that considers both short-term and long-term goals. This exercise encourages a sense of partnership and shared responsibility, fostering a resilient connection that can adapt to life's twists and turns.

Insight 8: **Practice Mindful Presence** Mindful presence is a powerful tool for cultivating a healthy balance in love. Being fully present in each moment allows partners to appreciate the richness of their shared experiences. Exercise: Integrate mindfulness practices into your daily routine, such as mindful breathing or shared moments of quiet reflection. Mindful presence enhances the quality of connection, fostering a sense of appreciation and gratitude within the relationship.

Insight 9: **Regularly Reflect on Relationship Dynamics** Regular self-reflection and mutual reflection on the dynamics of the relationship contribute to a healthy love balance. Partners can assess what is working well, identify areas for improvement, and set intentions for continued growth. Exercise: Schedule regular check-ins where you openly discuss the state of the relationship. This exercise promotes ongoing communication and ensures that both partners actively contribute to maintaining a balanced and fulfilling love connection.

Insight 10: **Nurture Intimacy Beyond the Physical** Intimacy is a multifaceted aspect of love that extends beyond the physical realm. Emotional, intellectual, and spiritual intimacy are equally vital for a healthy balance. Exercise: Engage in activities that foster emotional and intellectual connection, such as sharing thoughts, dreams, or engaging in joint creative pursuits. Nurturing diverse forms of intimacy enhances the depth and richness of the relationship.

Chapter 8: The Art of Letting Go: Mindful Release of Relationship Stress

Explore the difficulty of letting go of overthinking and stress in relationships

The difficulty of letting go of overthinking and stress in relationships is a multifaceted challenge that many individuals encounter in their journey toward healthier connections. Overthinking, often fueled by stress, can permeate the fabric of relationships, creating a barrier to genuine intimacy, effective communication, and emotional well-being. Understanding the roots of this difficulty and exploring strategies to release the grip of overthinking and stress is essential for fostering a more harmonious and fulfilling relationship.

The intricate nature of human psychology contributes to the challenge of letting go. Overthinking often arises from a complex interplay of past experiences, insecurities, and a natural tendency to anticipate and analyze potential outcomes. In relationships, this mental chatter can manifest as incessant questioning, doubt, and an overwhelming desire for certainty. The fear of the unknown and the need for reassurance can feed into the cycle of overthinking, making it challenging to release this habitual pattern.

Stress, whether originating from external sources or internal dynamics within the relationship, exacerbates the difficulty of letting go. The physiological and psychological impact of stress can amplify overthinking tendencies, creating a feedback loop that hinders the ability to find calmness and clarity. The body's stress response, characterized by heightened arousal and a focus on potential threats, can further entrench patterns of overthinking, making it challenging to break free from the cycle.

Insecurities and past traumas can also contribute to the reluctance to let go of overthinking and stress. Individuals who have experienced emotional wounds or betrayals may carry a heightened sensitivity to potential threats in their current relationships. The fear of being hurt again can intensify the need for control and certainty, fueling overthinking as a protective mechanism. Unraveling these deep-seated fears requires a willingness to confront past wounds and cultivate a sense of trust in oneself and the partner.

Social and cultural factors play a role in shaping the difficulty of letting go in relationships. Societal expectations, comparison with perceived relationship norms, and the fear of judgment can amplify the pressure to meet unrealistic standards. The desire to conform to external expectations may contribute to heightened stress and overthinking, as individuals grapple with the perceived need to navigate their relationships according to societal norms rather than authentic, individual needs.

Breaking free from the grip of overthinking and stress in relationships necessitates a commitment to self-awareness and intentional change. Mindfulness practices offer a powerful avenue for cultivating awareness of thought patterns and emotional responses. By bringing attention to the present moment without judgment, individuals can observe the fluctuations of the mind, creating space to disentangle from overthinking and stress-inducing thoughts.

Effective communication within the relationship is a key component of overcoming the difficulty of letting go. Partners can collaboratively establish open lines of communication where concerns, fears, and needs are expressed with vulnerability and empathy. Creating a safe space for transparent dialogue allows both individuals to share their experiences, fostering understanding and diminishing the need for overthinking.

Cognitive-behavioral techniques can be instrumental in reshaping thought patterns associated with overthinking. Identifying and challenging irrational or unproductive thoughts, known as cognitive restructuring, can interrupt the cycle of overthinking. Introducing realistic perspectives and alternative interpretations of situations helps shift the mindset, fostering a more balanced and constructive approach to relationship dynamics.

The cultivation of resilience is crucial in addressing the difficulty of letting go in relationships. Building emotional resilience involves developing coping strategies, practicing self-compassion, and embracing a growth mindset. Resilient individuals are better equipped to navigate challenges without succumbing to overthinking and stress. By fostering resilience, individuals can approach relationship difficulties with a sense of adaptability and optimism.

Letting go of overthinking and stress also requires a commitment to self-care. Prioritizing physical, emotional, and mental well-being contributes to a more balanced and centered mindset. Engaging in activities that promote relaxation, such as exercise, mindfulness, or hobbies, serves as a counterbalance to the demands of overthinking. Taking intentional breaks from relationship stressors allows individuals to recharge and approach challenges with a refreshed perspective.

Seeking professional support through therapy or counseling can be a transformative step in overcoming the difficulty of letting go. Therapists provide a neutral and supportive space for individuals and couples to explore the roots of overthinking, address underlying issues, and develop effective coping strategies. Professional guidance enhances self-awareness and equips individuals with the tools needed to navigate relationship dynamics more skillfully.

Cultivating a sense of acceptance is integral to the process of letting go. Acceptance involves acknowledging that uncertainties and challenges are inherent in relationships and, rather than trying to control every outcome, embracing the fluid nature of human connections. Acceptance creates space for flexibility, allowing individuals to release the need for constant overthinking and find peace in the present moment.

Principles of mindful release and acceptance

indful release and acceptance are foundational principles rooted in the practice of mindfulness, offering individuals a transformative approach to navigate the complexities of life with equanimity and presence. Embracing these principles involves cultivating a non-judgmental awareness of the present moment, letting go of attachment to outcomes, and acknowledging the impermanence of both joy and challenges. By delving into the principles of mindful release and acceptance, individuals can find a profound source of resilience and peace in the face of life's uncertainties.

At the core of mindful release is the recognition that suffering often arises from clinging to desires, expectations, and the illusion of control. Mindful release involves letting go of the grip of attachment to specific outcomes and embracing a more fluid and open-minded perspective. This principle encourages individuals to relinquish the need for situations to conform to preconceived notions, allowing space for life to unfold with its inherent unpredictability.

Acceptance, a companion to mindful release, involves acknowledging and embracing the reality of each moment without resistance. It's an active and intentional stance that goes beyond resignation; it's about making peace with what is. This doesn't imply passive acquiescence to challenging circumstances but rather a conscious choice to respond with equanimity, recognizing that resistance often amplifies suffering. Acceptance opens the door to a more compassionate engagement with oneself and the external world.

Mindful release and acceptance are deeply intertwined with the concept of impermanence. Everything in life is in a constant state of flux, and embracing this truth is central to the principles at hand. By recognizing that both joy and challenges are temporary, individuals can navigate life's ups and downs with a greater sense of ease. This awareness fosters a resilience that arises from a deep understanding that nothing is fixed or permanent.

Another aspect of mindful release and acceptance involves cultivating a non-judgmental awareness of thoughts and emotions. Mindfulness encourages individuals to observe their inner experiences without attaching labels of "good" or "bad." This non-judgmental awareness creates a space for self-compassion and a more objective understanding of one's internal landscape. It allows individuals to release the habitual patterns of self-criticism and cultivate a sense of inner peace.

Letting go of the past and future is a key component of mindful release and acceptance. Often, individuals carry the weight of past regrets or anxieties about the future, which can contribute to stress and overthinking. Mindfulness invites individuals to bring their attention to the present moment, where true peace and clarity reside. By releasing attachment to past narratives and future projections, individuals can free themselves from unnecessary mental burdens.

Mindful release and acceptance also involve cultivating gratitude for the present moment. Gratitude is a powerful antidote to dissatisfaction and overthinking. By appreciating the small joys and blessings in everyday life, individuals shift their focus from what is lacking to what is abundant. This shift in perspective contributes to a more positive and contented outlook, fostering a sense of fulfillment in the present.

The practice of mindful release and acceptance extends to interpersonal relationships. Embracing these principles in the context of relationships involves letting go of unrealistic expectations and accepting individuals as they are. It involves releasing the need to control or change others and fostering a space of understanding and compassion. By approaching relationships with mindful release and acceptance, individuals can cultivate healthier and more harmonious connections.

Mindful release and acceptance are not about passivity; rather, they empower individuals to respond skillfully to life's challenges. This responsiveness arises from a place of clarity and presence rather than reactive patterns driven by fear or aversion. The principles encourage individuals to pause, observe, and choose intentional responses, fostering a more skillful and compassionate way of engaging with the world.

The role of mindfulness practices, such as meditation and mindful breathing, is integral to the cultivation of mindful release and acceptance. These practices serve as vehicles for developing the capacity to be fully present in each moment, cultivating an awareness that extends beyond the habitual patterns of the mind. Regular mindfulness practice strengthens the neural pathways associated with mindful release and acceptance, making them more accessible in daily life.

Practical techniques for letting go of unnecessary worries and stress in love

Letting go of unnecessary worries and stress in love is a vital skill that contributes to the overall health and harmony of a relationship. When individuals can release the grip of unnecessary concerns, they create space for authentic connection, open communication, and a more fulfilling shared journey. Practical techniques for letting go of worries and stress in love encompass a range of mindfulness practices, communication strategies, and self-care approaches.

1. **Mindful Breathing:** Engaging in mindful breathing is a simple yet powerful technique for letting go of stress in love. Taking intentional, slow breaths helps activate the body's relaxation response, reducing the physiological and emotional impact of stress. When faced with worries or tension, individuals can pause and focus on their breath, bringing attention to the present moment and allowing the mind to settle.

2. **Mindful Awareness of Thoughts:** Mindfulness involves cultivating an awareness of thoughts without becoming entangled in them. When worries arise, individuals can practice observing these thoughts without judgment. This mindful awareness helps create a distance from the thoughts, allowing for a more objective and less emotionally charged perspective.

3. **Positive Visualization:** Visualization techniques can be effective in shifting focus from worries to positive outcomes. Individuals can mentally picture scenarios where their concerns are resolved or visualize moments of joy and

connection in their relationship. Positive visualization serves as a counterbalance to negative thinking, promoting a more optimistic outlook.

4. **Gratitude Practice:** Cultivating a gratitude practice is a transformative way to shift attention away from stressors. Regularly acknowledging and appreciating the positive aspects of the relationship fosters a sense of abundance and contentment. Gratitude can be expressed through journaling, verbal affirmations, or shared moments of appreciation with a partner.

5. **Effective Communication:** Open and honest communication is a fundamental tool for alleviating stress in love. When worries arise, expressing them to a partner fosters understanding and collaboration. Effective communication involves not only sharing concerns but also actively listening to a partner's perspective. This exchange creates a supportive environment where both individuals feel heard and valued.

6. **Setting Realistic Expectations:** Often, stress in relationships stems from unrealistic expectations. Individuals can mitigate this by setting realistic

expectations for themselves, their partner, and the relationship. Recognizing that perfection is unattainable and embracing the imperfections inherent in any relationship contributes to a more grounded and less stress-inducing mindset.

7. **Establishing Boundaries:** Clear boundaries are essential for maintaining a healthy balance and reducing unnecessary stress. Individuals can communicate and establish boundaries around personal space, alone time, and expectations. Respecting each other's boundaries creates a sense of safety and autonomy within the relationship, reducing potential sources of stress.

8. **Mindful Time Management:** Effectively managing time and priorities contributes to stress reduction. Couples can collaborate on creating schedules that allow for both individual pursuits and shared activities. Mindful time management ensures that responsibilities are shared equitably and that each partner has the space to attend to their needs, promoting a more balanced and stress-free dynamic.

9. **Self-Care Rituals:** Prioritizing self-care is a crucial component of stress reduction in love. Individuals can establish self-care rituals that nourish their physical, emotional, and mental well-being. Whether it's taking a relaxing bath, engaging in a favorite hobby, or spending time in nature, self-care practices contribute to resilience and a more positive mindset.

10. **Practice Acceptance:** Letting go of worries involves accepting the reality of the present moment. Acceptance doesn't imply resignation but rather acknowledging that certain aspects of the relationship are beyond one's control. Practicing acceptance allows individuals to release the grip of unnecessary stressors and approach challenges with a more adaptable and grounded mindset.

11. **Mindful Reflection:** Regular reflection on one's thoughts and emotions contributes to self-awareness. Individuals can set aside time for mindful reflection, exploring the root causes of their worries and stress. This intentional self-inquiry fosters a deeper understanding of underlying concerns and provides insights into potential solutions.

12. **Engaging in Relaxation Techniques:**
    Incorporating relaxation techniques, such
    as progressive muscle relaxation or
    guided imagery, can help release physical
    tension associated with stress. These
    techniques promote a state of calmness
    and relaxation, creating a physiological
    counterbalance to the stress response.

Conclusion: Embracing Mindful Love for Lasting Connection

Key principles and strategies for addressing overthinking in relationships

Addressing overthinking in relationships involves applying key principles and strategies to foster a healthier and more balanced dynamic. Mindful love serves as the guiding philosophy, emphasizing present-moment awareness, non-judgmental understanding, and intentional connection. Here's a concise summary of the key principles and strategies:

1. Mindful Awareness: Central to addressing overthinking is cultivating mindful awareness. This involves being fully present in the current moment without getting entangled in intrusive thoughts about the past or future. Mindful awareness provides a foundation for understanding one's thought patterns and emotions, allowing individuals to respond to relationship challenges with greater clarity.

2. Non-Judgmental Understanding: Overthinking often involves harsh self-criticism and judgment. Adopting a non-judgmental stance towards oneself and the partner is crucial. Instead of labeling

thoughts as "good" or "bad," individuals can practice observing them without attachment. This principle encourages self-compassion and promotes a more empathetic understanding of the complexities within the relationship.

3. Effective Communication: Open and honest communication is a cornerstone for addressing overthinking. Partners can create a safe space for expressing thoughts and concerns without fear of judgment. Actively listening to each other fosters mutual understanding, reducing the likelihood of misinterpretations and conflicts driven by overthinking.

4. Setting Healthy Boundaries: Establishing clear and healthy boundaries is essential for managing overthinking. Boundaries help individuals define their personal space, needs, and limits. Communicating and respecting these boundaries creates a sense of security within the relationship, reducing the need to overanalyze or control every aspect.

5. Cultivating Gratitude: Gratitude serves as a powerful antidote to overthinking. Focusing on the positive aspects of the relationship and expressing gratitude for each other's contributions create a more

optimistic mindset. This shift in perspective reinforces a sense of abundance and fulfillment, diminishing the tendency to dwell on potential problems.

6. Mindful Decision-Making: Mindful decision-making involves making choices based on present-moment awareness rather than reactive patterns driven by overthinking. Partners can collaborate on decisions, considering each other's perspectives and the impact on the relationship. Mindful decision-making reduces the likelihood of unnecessary worry about future outcomes.

7. Self-Reflection: Regular self-reflection is key to addressing overthinking. Individuals can explore the root causes of their overthinking tendencies, identifying patterns and triggers. This introspective practice enhances self-awareness, empowering individuals to break free from habitual overthinking and make conscious choices within the relationship.

8. Conflict Resolution with Empathy: Overthinking can contribute to communication breakdowns and conflicts. Resolving conflicts with empathy involves actively listening to

each other's concerns, validating emotions, and seeking collaborative solutions. This approach fosters a deeper connection and minimizes the impact of overthinking on relationship dynamics.

9. Mindful Presence in Intimacy: Mindful presence extends to intimate moments in the relationship. Being fully present during shared experiences fosters a deeper emotional connection and reduces distractions caused by overthinking. Couples can practice mindful intimacy to enhance the quality of their connection.

10. Continuous Growth and Learning: Embracing the idea that relationships are a journey of continuous growth and learning helps individuals navigate challenges with resilience. Rather than viewing obstacles as insurmountable, partners can approach them as opportunities for personal and relational development, reducing the burden of overthinking.

Embrace mindful love as a lifelong practice

Embracing mindful love as a lifelong practice is an invitation to transform the way individuals engage in relationships, fostering a deep and enduring sense of connection. Mindful love goes beyond fleeting romantic gestures; it becomes a guiding philosophy, a way of being that permeates every aspect of one's interactions with oneself and others. Here are compelling reasons to encourage readers to embark on the journey of mindful love as a lifelong practice:

Mindful love is an ongoing journey of self-discovery. As individuals commit to the practice of mindfulness within the context of relationships, they embark on a profound exploration of their own thoughts, emotions, and patterns of behavior. This self-awareness lays the foundation for personal growth, allowing individuals to cultivate a deeper understanding of their needs, desires, and responses in the realm of love.

In the pursuit of mindful love, individuals learn to navigate the ebb and flow of relationships with grace and resilience. Rather than viewing challenges as insurmountable obstacles, they embrace them as opportunities for growth and learning. Mindful love encourages a mindset of adaptability and open-heartedness, fostering an environment where relationships can evolve and flourish over time.

Embracing mindful love is an antidote to the pitfalls of overthinking and unnecessary worries. By staying rooted in the present moment, individuals release the burden of ruminating on the past or anxiously anticipating the future. This practice allows for a more genuine and spontaneous connection with a partner, free from the constraints of overanalyzing every interaction.

Mindful love promotes a culture of deep appreciation and gratitude. Individuals who engage in this lifelong practice consistently recognize and celebrate the positive aspects of their relationships. Gratitude becomes a cornerstone, fostering an environment where partners feel seen, valued, and cherished. This intentional focus on appreciation contributes to a more positive and fulfilling love experience.

The principles of mindful love extend beyond romantic partnerships to encompass relationships with family, friends, and oneself. It becomes a holistic approach to connection, emphasizing the importance of being fully present in every interaction. By embracing mindful love in all relationships, individuals create a ripple effect of authenticity, compassion, and understanding that positively impacts their entire social network.

A lifelong commitment to mindful love involves an ongoing exploration of the nuances of intimacy. Partners engaged in this practice continually deepen their emotional connection through mindful presence in shared experiences. From mundane moments to significant milestones, the practice of mindful love enriches the fabric of the relationship, creating a tapestry woven with intention and authenticity.

Mindful love serves as a guiding light during moments of conflict and misunderstanding. Instead of reacting impulsively, individuals grounded in mindful love approach conflicts with a spirit of empathy and active listening. This approach transforms disagreements into opportunities for mutual understanding, strengthening the bonds of the relationship.

The lifelong practice of mindful love is an investment in emotional well-being. It nurtures a sense of inner peace and contentment, reducing the impact of external stressors on the relationship. By prioritizing self-care and maintaining a balanced mindset, individuals contribute to the creation of a resilient and thriving love connection.

Ultimately, encouraging readers to embrace mindful love as a lifelong practice is an invitation to embark on a transformative journey of personal and relational growth. It is a commitment to building relationships that are not only enduring but also deeply fulfilling. Through the practice of mindful love, individuals cultivate a love that is intentional, authentic, and capable of withstanding the tests of time.

Final thoughts on the transformative power of mindfulness in fostering lasting connection and fulfillment in relationships

In reflecting on the transformative power of mindfulness in fostering lasting connection and fulfillment in relationships, one cannot help but marvel at the profound impact this practice can have on the fabric of human connections. Mindfulness, as a way of being, transcends the ordinary and becomes a catalyst for extraordinary transformations within the realm of relationships.

At its core, mindfulness invites individuals to be fully present in each moment, to engage in a conscious and non-judgmental awareness of themselves and their partners. This intentional presence serves as the cornerstone of authentic connection, allowing individuals to show up in relationships with a clarity that goes beyond surface interactions. As couples embark on the journey of mindful connection, they discover a depth of understanding and a richness of experience that transcends the superficial.

The transformative power of mindfulness lies in its ability to reshape the dynamics of communication. Mindful listening, characterized by a genuine openness to the partner's words, fosters an environment of trust and vulnerability. Through this deepened communication, couples forge bonds that withstand the tests of time. The practice of mindful communication becomes a tool for resolving conflicts with compassion, paving the way for a more harmonious and resilient connection.

Mindfulness is a beacon of light during the storms of life, offering solace and resilience in the face of challenges. Rather than succumbing to the pressures of external stressors, couples grounded in mindfulness approach difficulties with a sense of shared purpose and adaptability. The ability to navigate life's ups and downs with equanimity becomes a testament to the strength of the connection forged through mindful love.

The transformative journey of mindfulness in relationships extends beyond the couple to impact the broader community. As individuals cultivate mindfulness within themselves and with their partners, they contribute to a collective consciousness of compassion and understanding. This ripple effect has the potential to create a more interconnected and harmonious social fabric, fostering a world where mindful relationships serve as beacons of inspiration.

Fulfillment in relationships is intricately linked to the practice of gratitude within the framework of mindfulness. Partners who consciously express gratitude for each other's presence, contributions, and uniqueness create a positive and affirming atmosphere. This intentional focus on gratitude becomes a source of nourishment, sustaining the emotional well-being of the individuals and the relationship as a whole.

In essence, the transformative power of mindfulness in relationships lies in its capacity to elevate the ordinary to the extraordinary. Mundane moments become infused with meaning, and daily interactions take on a profound significance. Mindfulness is a reminder that love is not merely a destination but a journey—a journey of exploration, growth, and shared experiences.

As we contemplate the impact of mindfulness on lasting connection and fulfillment in relationships, it becomes evident that this practice is not a fleeting trend but a timeless and universal truth. Mindfulness has the potential to revolutionize how individuals approach love, guiding them toward a path of depth, authenticity, and enduring connection. The journey of mindful love is an ongoing evolution, a dance of presence and awareness that transforms relationships into sanctuaries of joy, understanding, and profound fulfillment.